PANTHEISTICON

D1871320

Owing to the antiquity and rarity of this book, certain pages are regrettably absent, and readability is compromised due to the blurring of the original text. If you possess any insights regarding the availability of these missing sections, kindly inform us. Your assistance is crucial in ensuring the completion of this significant work for the benefit of future generations.

PANTHEISTICON

The Form of Celebrating the Socratic-Society. Divided Into Three Parts. Which Contain, I. The Morals and Axioms Of The Pantheists; Or The Brotherhood; II. Their Deity and Philosophy; III. Their Liberty, And A Law, Neither Deceiving, Nor

John Toland

GYAN

Published by

Gyan Publishing House
5, Ansari Road
Daryaganj, New Delhi-110002
Phone: 011-47034999, 9811692060
E-mail: books@gyanbooks.com

Distribution Network
gyanbooks.com
India, USA, Canada, UK, Australia

© Publisher

All rights reserved. No part of this work may be reproduced, stored, adapted, or transmitted in any form or by any means, electronic, mechanical, photocopying, micro-filming, recording or otherwise, or translated in any language, without the prior written permission of the copyright owner and the publisher.

ISBN: 978-93-6208-121-6 (PB)
First Published, 1751

2nd Impression 2024

Printed at: Gyan Press, Delhi.

The book is sold subject to the condition that it shall not, by way of trade or otherwise, be lent, resold, hired out, or otherwise circulated without the prior publisher's written consent.

PANTHEISTICON
Author: JOHN TOLAND

Pantheisticon:

OR, THE

FORM

Of Celebrating the

Socratic - Society.

Divided into THREE PARTS.

Which Contain,

I. The MORALS and AXIOMS of the PANTHEISTS; or the BROTHERHOOD.

II. Their Deity and Philosophy.

III. Their Liberty, and a Law, neither deceiving, nor to be deceived.

To which is prefix'd

A DISCOURSE upon the Antient and Modern Societies of the LEARNED, as also upon the Infinite and Eternal UNIVERSE.

And subjoined,

A short DISSERTATION, upon a Two-fold Philosophy of the PANTHEISTS, that is to be followed; together with an Idea of the best and most accomplished MAN.

Written Originally in LATIN, by the INGENIOUS Mr. *JOHN TOLAND*.

And now, for the first Time, faithfully rendered into ENGLISH.

LONDON

Printed for SAM. PATERSON, at *Shakespear's-Head*, opposite *Durham-Yard*, in the *Strand*: and Sold by

ET IDEM
James Bindley

* *Janus Junius Eoganesius,*

TO THE

LEARNED and INGENIOUS

READER.

AS *one, who has the Interest of Mankind greatly at Heart, and as a strict Votary of the eternal Truth, I present to you, (candid Reader) a* New Fellowship *and*

 New

* Mr. *Toland* was born in the most Northern Peninsula of *Ireland*, in the Isthmus of *Londonderry*. —That Peninsula was originally called, *Inis-Eogan*, or *Inis-Eogain*; but it is now called, *Inisoen*, or *Inis-Owen*. He was christened *Janus Junius*, whence he calls himself *Janus Junius Eoganesius*. —See Memoirs of his Life and Writings.

New Regulation; *by the embracing of which, you shall not only become better and wiser, but even live a Life of Joy, a Life of Happiness and Contentment. By what Chance, or Care, these Things have been now brought to Light, it neither is my Business to tell you, nor does it concern you to know. For to form a competent Judgment of them, our sole View must be directed towards themselves, we must even consult nothing but themselves, as no extrinsic Estimation, much less Authority, can enhance their Value. The Generality of Mankind is averse from Knowledge, and vents Invectives against its Partizans; but as* Seneca *nobly instructs us,* To use our utmost Efforts, that Cattle-like, we might not follow the Herd of those that go before; going not where we should go, but where they go. *And in a few Lines after,* Since every Man chuses rather to believe than judge, Life then is never brought to a Scrutiny, Credulity has always

De vita beata, Cap. 1.

always the Aſcendant, Error handed down from Father to Son embarraſſes our Thoughts in its Mazes, we give headlong into it: In a word, it is the dull Infatuation of being led by the Examples of others, that expoſes us to Ruin. *What therefore remains to be done?* We ſhall be in Safety, *(ſays* Ibid. Cap. *he)* if we ſeparate ourſelves from the 2. Multitude; for the Multitude *(as the ſame Author inculcates a little after)* is a Proof of what is worſt. And nothing is ſo vulgar, *(in the Opinion of* Tully) as to have no Reliſh for Know- De divi- ledge. nat. lib. 2. Cap. 39.

Philoſophy *(to make ſtill Uſe of* Tuſc. Diſ- Tully's *Words)* contents itſelf with a few put. Lib. Judges; it deſignedly ſhuns the Mul- 2. Cap. 1. titude, as conſcious of its Jealouſy and Hatred; ſo that ſhould one undertake to vilify and caſt an Odium upon Philoſophy in general, he may do it with the Approbation of the People; or, ſhould

ſhould he ſtrive to attack the Philoſophy that we adhere to, he may find great Reſources in the Syſtems of other Philoſophers. *For your Part, Reader, if you chuſe to follow* Reaſon, *rather than* Cuſtom, *for your Guide, you ſhall repute all Human Caſualties to be placed in a Degree far beneath you; you ſhall patiently take up with your Lot, whatever it is; you ſhall keep at a Diſtance from you fooliſh Ambition, and gnawing Envy; you ſhall deſpiſe periſhable Honours, being to periſh yourſelf in a ſhort Time; you ſhall lead a peaceable and pleaſant Life, neither admiring nor dreading any Thing; and you ſhall deſervedly apply to yourſelf theſe Verſes of* Virgil,

Georg. Lib. ii, Ver. 490.

Felix qui potuit rerum cognoſcere cauſas,
Atque metus omnes & inexorabile fatum
Subjecit pedibus, ſtrepitumque Acherontis avari.

—— Bleſt

To the READER.

——————— Blest the Man!
Who could of Things the secret Causes
trace;
And cast all Fears, and Fate's unmoved
Decree,
And roaring *Acheron*, beneath his Feet.

TRAPP.

Be such by reading this PANTHEISTICON: *And when you know that it is a Philosophical, and not a Theological Description, that's here given of the Society, (for there's a wide Difference between unfolding Nature's Mysteries, and discoursing on Religion) I shall bid you be wise, and*

Farewell.

OF THE ANTIENT and MODERN SOCIETIES OF THE LEARNED.

AS ALSO A DISSERTATION upon the Infinite and Eternal UNIVERSE.

I.

MAN, as a ſociable Animal, can neither live well, nor happy, nor at any rate, without the Help and Concurrence of Others; therefore ſeveral Societies, nay innumerable, neceſſarily aroſe from the very Nature

of

of the Thing. Husbands enter into a ſtrict Alliance with Wives, Parents with Children, Maſters with Servants, Magiſtrates with Subjects, and finally, from the coming together of all thoſe Men, with their reſpective Families, the Union of living in Cities is formed. Some of theſe Societies are more, others leſs voluntary. The former, of which we ſpeak here, were called by the antient *Greeks* and *Romans*, *Brotherhoods*, *Friendſhips*, *Fellowſhips*, *Societies*. The latter too, affect very often the ſame Appellation; but we are not to treat here of the Corporations of Merchants and Artizans, nor of religious Communities, and political Aſſemblies; ſuch were the *Arval Brethren*, *Titian Companions*, *Auguſtals*, *Flavials*, and *Antoniniani*. What we ſpeak of, are thoſe Societies that were frequently inſtituted among the *Greeks* and *Romans*, either for the Pleaſure or Inſtruction of the Mind. Religious Aſſemblies, eſpecially if held in the Night-time, and all others, either running upon Politics, or intereſting themſelves in any Shape with Regard to the Commonwealth, were often reſtrained

Φρατρίαι, ἑταιρία ἤ ἑταιρεία. Sodalitia, Sodalitates.

ed and prohibited by the Laws; as alſo thoſe ſolemn Regalios, many of which were celebrated on ſtated Days of the Year, to ſay nothing of the Companies of Artificers, that are vaſtly different from ours. This Misfortune, or Diſgrace, ſeldom or ever befel learned Fraternities, friendly and facetious Banquets, which were called by the *Greeks*, * *Sympoſia* and *Syndeipna*, by the *Latins*, ‡ *Compotationes* and *Concœnationes*, not unlike the *Suſſitia* of the *Spartans*. Each Member of the Society contributed ſomething towards the Supper, that was to be in common; this Contribution was called by the *Greeks*, *Symbolum* or *Symbola*; by the *Romans*, to uſe *Cicero*'s Term, *Collecta*, from whence the Entertainment itſelf was called, *Cœna Collatitia*; thoſe who contributed nothing were *Aſymboli*, *i.e.* Scot-free. The *Symbolum* moreover was called by the

It may be that the Author alludes here to the Company of Free-Maſons.

Συσσίτια.

Σύμβολον Συμβολή. A Club.

Ἀσύμβολοι.

B 2 *Greeks*,

* Συμπόσια, Σύνδειπνα. ‡ Compotationes, Concœnationes, — are ſynonimous Terms, to ſignify Eating and Drinking in Community.

Greeks, † *Eranium*, the Supper *Eranos*, the Guests *Eranistæ*, and the Master of the Feast *Eranarcha*.

II.

BUT as nothing in Nature is more beautiful than Disposition and Order, so, in all such Banquets, the Brethren, who, for the most Part, should not be more in Number than the Muses, nor fewer than the Graces, or rather the exact Number of the Planets, chuse among themselves, by casting the Dice, a *President*, who might point out for them the Order of Drinking and Argument. This *President* was also characterized with several other Titles, as the *Manager of the Club*, the *Chief*, the *Umpire*, the *King*, the *Captain-General*, the *Father of the Supper*, the *Lord of the Banquet*, the *Master of the Revels*, according to *Cicero*; and, according to *Varro*, the *Steward of the*

'Εταῖροι.

Επίσταθμος.

Συμποσίαρχος, Στρατηγος, Βασιλεὺς. Magister Bibendi, Modiperator.

† Ἐράνιον ἔρανος. ἐρανισαὶ, ἐρανάρχης. — These Words signify, also, Tribute-money, the Collectors of Taxes, Charity extended to needy Friends, and the Stone called the *Turquoise*.

the Feast. For which Reason, *Jupiter Good-fellow* was worshipped under that Name, as the most equitable Mediator and Arbitrator of the Laws of social Life. Whoever is willing to know the Qualities that are requisite for a good *President*, must consult at leisure the fourth Question of the first Book of *Plutarch*'s *Symposia*, for they regard rather the Laws of Drinking than Argument. Now as these Banquets were *seasonable* or *unseasonable*, more or less delicate and sumptuous, those which *Hermogenes* calls, *Socratic Entertainments*, easily bore the Sway over all others, and were justly more commendable. We have a Specimen of them in the Writings of the two most excellent Disciples of the divine *Socrates*, to wit, *Plato* and *Zenophon*.

*Ἑταιρεῖος Ζεύς.

Συμπόσια Σωκρατικά.

III.

OUR Age likewise has produced not a few, who, at Table, desirous to dispute freely, and with less Restraint, upon any Topic whatsoever, instituted

instituted Entertainments, not unlike those of the *Socratics*, and even called them, not improperly, *Socratic Societies.* Most of these are Philosophers, or, at least, in a Degree bordering upon Philosophers: Bigotted to no one's Opinion, nor led aside by Education or Custom, nor subservient to the Religion and Laws of their Country; they freely and impartially, in the Silence of all Prejudices, and with the greatest Sedateness of Mind, discuss and bring to a Scrutiny all Things, as well sacred (as the saying is) as prophane. They are called, for the most Part, *Pantheists*, upon Account of an Opinion concerning GOD and the UNIVERSE, peculiar to themselves; but diametrically opposite to the *Epicureans*, *Chaologists*, and *Oneiropolists*, as they acknowledge no first Confusion, no Fortune, much less Chance, to be the Maker of the World. Notwithstanding they deliver their Sentiments, concerning the Cause and Origin of Things, in Conjunction with *Linus*, the most antient, most authentic, and revered Oracle of mysterious Science, saying,

In the A-

In the Analogy of the Term, the *Pantheists* are more opposed to *Atheists*; but Use, that great Master of Language will have it otherwise.

All

† *All Things are from the Whole, and the Whole is from all Things.*

This ſhort Sentence, which they always have in their Mouth, requires to be fully explained, wherefore we ſhall here briefly clear it up, by adjuſting exactly Words to Things.

They aſſert that the Univerſe (of which this World we behold with our Eyes is but a ſmall Portion) is infinite both in Extenſion and Virtue, but one, in the Continuation of the Whole, and Contiguity of the Parts: Immoveable according to the Whole, as beyond it there's no Place or Space, but moveable according to the Parts, or by Diſtances in Number infinite: Incorruptible and neceſſary both Ways, to wit, *eternal in Exiſtence and Duration: Intelligent alſo by an eminent Reaſon, and not to receive its Denomination from our intellectual Faculty, unleſs by a ſlight Similitude: Finally, whoſe integrant Parts are always the ſame, and conſtituent Parts always in Motion.*

I

† Ἐκ παντὸς δὲ τὰ παντα, καὶ ἐκ παντων τὸ πᾶν ἐστι. — All Things are from the All, and the All is from all Things. STOB. *Eclog. Phyſ.*

I could not expreſs theſe Things in ſo conciſe a manner, with greater Perſpicuity, yet for the further Satisfaction of the Reader, I ſhall animadvert upon them, one after another.

IV.

FROM that Motion and Intellect that conſtitute the Force and Harmony of the infinite Whole, innumerable Species of Things ariſe, every Individual of which is both a Matter and Form to itſelf, Form being nothing elſe than a Diſpoſition of Parts in each Body From whence therefore we may conclude, that the beſt Reaſon, and moſt perfect Order, regulate all Things in the *Univerſe*, in which there are infinite Worlds, diſtinguiſhed from one another, as other Parts by their peculiar Attributes, although, with Regard to the Whole, there are no Parts really ſeparate. Things moving by Parts in no wiſe take away from the Perfection of the *Univerſe*, as thereby new Perfections are produced, by a never-ceaſing Principle

ciple of Generation. Neither is the constant Dissolution of many Things, that result from those Parts, an Hindrance to its Perfection, inasmuch as this is a Point of the greatest Perfection; for nothing of the Whole perishes, but Destruction and Production succeed each other by turns, and all by a perpetual Change of Forms, and a certain most beautiful Variety and Vicissitude of Things, operate necessarily towards the Participation, Good, and Preservation of the Whole, and make, as it were, an everlasting Circulation.

That grow together from those Parts.

* That celebrated Darling of the Muses was of Opinion, *That from One all Things are made, and shall be reunited to the same.* Finally, the Force and Energy of the Whole, the Creator and Ruler of All, and always tending to the best End, is GOD, whom you may call the *Mind*, if you please, and *Soul* of the Universe; and hence it is, that the *Socratic Brethren*, by a pecu-

C liar

---

* Diogen. Laert. in proœmio, Sect. 3. ἐξ ἑνὸς τὰ παντα γενέσθαι, και εἰς ταὐτὸν αναλύεσθαι. Out of One all Things sprung, and are to be dissolved into, and confounded with, the same again.

liar Term, as I said before, are called PANTHEISTS; this Force, according to them, being not separated from the *Universe* itself, but by a Distinction of Reason alone. *Gregory* of *Ariminum*, *Occhamus*, *Cajetanus*, *Thomas Aquinas* even, who was canonized, to pass by Others, thought not that they contradicted the *Mosaic Formation of the World*, neither do I, when they taught,
Cosmopœia. *That God was the eternal Cause of the eternal World, and that all Things, from all Eternity, flowed from God without a Medium*; but *Jerom* thinks finely upon
In Isai. lxvi. 1. the Matter, where he says, *That God is infused and circumfused, both within and without the World.* And this is the Sentiment of the antient Philosophers, especially of the *Pythagorics*.

V.

TO set still, in a clearer Light, the Manner of the PANTHEIST's Philosophizing, I say, that the first Bodies, or the Elements (if I am allowed the Expression of the Elements) are most

most simple, and actually indivisible, infinite too in Number and Species, and that all Things are made out of their Composition, Separation, and various Mixture, but with proper Measures, Weights, and Motions; to wit, with a mutual and mechanic Proportion and Disproportion of Parts in their Nature moveable, and with a mutual Determination of concurring and impelling Bodies, which without any Void are divided into their own Elements. There is no Intermission of Determinations, inasmuch as there is no Space void, **Vacuum.** nor a last Barrier. For the commonly received Axiom in Schools, viz. *There's no such Thing as a Progress of Motion* in infinitum, is both sophistical and false, as there are infinite Individuals, and as neither a First nor a Last can be fixed upon; and though we willingly grant, that there is no infinite Determination, or any particular Species of Motion; yet, at the same time, we make no Allowance for a first corporeal Moveable, or an immovable Center of the *Universe*, or even a Center of the *Universe*, in any Sense whatsoever. As to the Devices of *Epicurus*, who asserted, *That these Things were cemented, and concreted together, by rough and smooth, and hooked and crooked Bodies, not forgetting the Interposition of his Void*, we shall leave them to himself, with his fortuitous Concourse of Atoms, and Declination of the same not extrinsically determined; acting, perhaps, something in his Distances between divers Worlds; that we should not dwell long upon the eternal Descent of Atoms to a Line, and such like Paralogisms, when in an infinite Space, neither the highest nor the lowest, nor the middle nor the last, can be conceived. Internal and universal Action, the chiefest of all Motions, is circumscribed by no Limits, the *Universe* itself being unlimited, wherefore there will be no Absurdity in establishing an infinite Action; but all particular Motions mutually terminate, restrain, retard, or accelerate themselves, according to the Manner and Strength of every Resistance or Impulse. Our Design does not permit us to dispute here, either upon the mutual Action of the Globes against themselves, or upon Arguments

guments in Defence of a Void, which have been advanced by Philoſophers of no ſmall Repute. Whoever feeds his Fancy with theſe Notions, let him conſult the great *Newton*. In compounded Bodies are contained, as we ſaid, Particles of every Species, that cannot be cut or parted, this or that Species having the Aſcendant, for *the more there is in a Thing of the Subſtance of another*, (according to the old Maxim) *the more it will derive from it its Appellation*; ſo that, it comes to paſs, that there's no real Innovation in the World, except the ſole Permutation of Place, from whence proceed the Production and Deſtruction of all Things, *to wit*, by Generation, Encreaſe, Alteration, and ſuch like Motions. For all Things, as we already remarked, are in Motion, and all Diverſities whatſoever are ſo many Names for particular Motions, not one ſingle Point in Nature being abſolutely at reſt, but only with regard to other Things, Reſt itſelf being truly and eſſentially a Motion of Reſiſtance,

VI.

THOUGHT, which we muſt not omit ſpeaking of, is a peculiar Motion of the Brain, the proper Organ of this Faculty; or rather a certain Part of the Brain continued in the * Spinal Marrow, and in the Nerves with their † Membranes, conſtitutes the principal Seat of the Soul, and performs the Motion both of Thought and Senſation; which vary wonderfully, according to the different Structure of the Brain, in all Kinds of Animals. As to other Movements of the Body, performed by the Means of the Nerves, we undertake not here to ſpeak of them.

The Ethereal Fire environing all Things, and therefore ſupreme; permeating all Things, and therefore intimate, of which a Kitchen Fire is a certain analogical and imperfect Similitude; the

* The Spinal Marrow that begins in the Brain, and runs along the Ridge of the Back.

† *Meninx*, a thin Membrane which incloſeth the Brains, whereof there are two, the one thicker, called *Dura Mater*, the other thinner, called *Pia Mater*.

the Ether, I say, by a wonderful Structure of the Brain thereunto adjusted, and by exterior Objects that act on the Brain, through the Means of the Nerves of the Senses, and excite therein various Imaginations, duly executes all the Machinery of Conception, Imagination, Remembrance, Amplification, and Diminution of Ideas. It is this Fire alone, more fleet than Thought itself, and by far more subtil than any other Kind of Matter, which can with so quick a Motion run over the tended Cords and Ligaments of the Nerves, and variously agitate them, according to the different Impressions of Objects upon the Nerves. What is more, the Ether is a reviving Fire, infusing a sweet and gentle Warmth, not burning, not dissipating, not consuming as ordinary Fire. * *It rules all Things*, (says the Author of the Treatise upon Diet) *it disposes of all Things, according to Nature, without Noise, and im-*

Filaments
Threads

* ——πῦρ ὅπερ πάντων επικρατέεται, διέπει ἄπαντα κατὰ φύσιν, ἄψοφον και ὄψει και ψαύσει: εν τόυτω ψυχὴ, νόος, φρονησις, ἀυξησις, κίνησις, μείωσις, διάλλαξις, ὕπνος, εγρήγορσις: τοῦτο πάντα διὰ παντὸς κυβερνᾶ; καὶ τάδε καὶ εκεῖνα ὀυδέποτε ατρεμιζον. *Lib.* i. *Sect.* 11.

imperceptible, either to the Sight or Touch. In it is Soul, Mind, Prudence, Encrease, Motion, Diminution, Alteration, Sleep, Watching, it governs All in all Things, and never suffers celestial and terrestial Beings to be at Rest. This Fire is *Horace*'s *Particle of divine Breath*, and *Virgil*'s *inwardly nourishing Spirit, heavenly Origin, fiery Vigour*, and if there be any other Name, which he uses to express it. *The Animal Spirits* of the Moderns, and their *Liquidity of Nerves*, are but empty Titles, unless they denote this Fire. Now by what Means Imaginations are excited, or Ideas formed in the Brain (which Organ, as it is corporeal and very complex, it can produce nothing but what is corporeal) we made to appear in our second Book of *Esoterics*, where we demonstrated that all Ideas whatsoever are corporeal.

Internal Operations.

Wherefore rejecting the Notions of some, who figure to themselves the † *Diaphragm*, to be the Seat of the Soul, or the Heart, or Liver, or other Parts; *It*

† The Membrane that parteth the Heart and Lungs from the other Intrails.

* *It behoves Men to know,* (ſays *Hippocrates,* or rather *Democritus,* in that valuable Treatiſe upon the Falling Sickneſs) *that no other Part but the Brain affords us Pleaſures, as Mirth, Laughter, Diverſion; and, on the other Hand, Grief, Anxiety, Sadneſs, and Mourning: By its Means we become wiſe, and underſtand, and ſee, and hear, and know what's baſe and honeſt, good and bad, agreeable and diſagreeable, diſcerning ſome of them by Rule, and perceiving others by the Advantage that is annexed to*

Quod Sacræ Partis, *i.e.* Animi ſit. *Sacer Morbus,* ſo called.

D

* Εἰδέναι δὲ χρὴ ἀνθρώπους, ὅτι ἐξ οὐδενὸς ἡμῖν αἱ ἡδοναὶ γίνονται, καὶ αἱ εὐφροσύναι, καὶ γέλωτες, καὶ παιδιαὶ, ἢ ἐντεῦθεν: καὶ λῦπαι, καὶ ἀνίαι, καὶ δυσφροσύναι, καὶ κλαυθμοί. Καὶ τουτῳ φρονεῦμεν μάλιστα καὶ νοεῦμεν, καὶ βλέπομεν, καὶ ακούομεν, καὶ γινώσκομεν τάτε αἰσχρὰ καὶ τα καλά, καὶ τὰ κακὰ, καὶ αγαθά καὶ ἡδέα καὶ ἀηδέα; τα μὲν νομῳ διακρίνοντες, τὰδε τῳ συμφεροντι αἰσθανόμενοι. Τῳ δὲ τὰς ἡδονὰς καὶ τὰς ἀηδίας τοῖσι καιροῖσι διαγινώσκοντες, καὶ οὐ ταυτὰ ἀρέσκει ἡμῖν. Τῳ δὲ αὐτῳ τούτῳ καὶ μαινόμεθα καὶ παραφρονέομεν, καὶ δείματα καὶ φόβοι παρίστανται ἡμῖν, τὰ μὲν νύκταρ, τὰ δὲ μεθ᾽ ἡμέρην: καὶ ἐνύπνια καὶ πλάνοι ἄκαιροι, καὶ φροντίδες οὐχ ἱκνεύμεναι, καὶ ἄγνοσιν τῶν καθεστεώτων, καὶ ἀηθίη, καὶ ἀπειρίη. Καὶ ταῦτα πάσχομεν ἀπὸ τοῦ ἐγκεφάλου πάντα, ὅταν οὗτος μὴ υγιαίνῃ: αλλ᾽ ἢ θερμότερος τῆς φύσιος γενήται, ἢ ψυχρότερος, ἢ ὑγρότερος, ἢ ξηρότερος, ἢ τι ἄλλο πεπόνθῃ πάθος παρὰ τὴν φυσιν, ὃ μὴ εἰώθῃ. *Sect.* 16. The *Sections* 17 and 19 ſhould alſo be read, or rather the whole Book.

to them: By the ſame, in their proper Times, we diſtinguiſh Pleaſures from what are not ſo, and the ſame Things pleaſe us not always: By the ſame we grow delirious and run mad, we nurſe Terrors and Fears, ſome haunting us by Night, others by Day, our Thoughts are taken up with Dreams, we give into unſeaſonable Errors, we are poſſeſſed by empty Cares, we are ignorant of Standers-by, and we fall into a Diſuſe and Forgetfulneſs of Things. All this is occaſioned by the Brain, when it is not in its due Poſition; that is to ſay, when it is not ſound, but is hotter or colder, moiſter or dryer, or, in fine, ſuffers any Thing contrary to what is natural or uſual. The Tongue is not more the Organ of the Taſte, than the Brain is that of Thought: But let our Diſcourſe return to the Place from whence it has digreſſed.

VII.

VII.

THE Seeds of all Things, begun from an eternal Time, are composed out of the first Bodies, or most simple Principles, the four commonly received Elements being neither simple nor sufficient: For in an Infinity all Things are infinite, nay even eternal, as nothing could be made out of nothing, and therefore we may conclude, that the organic Structure of Seeds could not be formed out of any Concourse of Atoms, or any Species of Motion whatsoever. To illustrate this Tenet by some Example or other, the Seed of a Tree is not alone in Power a Tree, according to the Notion of *Aristotle*; but a real Tree, in which are all the integrant Parts of a Tree, though so minute, as not to be perceived by the Senses without Microscopes, and not even then, but in a very few Things. All that this Tree wants is a fuller Distinction and Magnitude of Parts, which is gradually acquired by the Application

Potentia, capable of becoming a Tree, or in a Possibility of being a Tree.

of ſimple Bodies of diſtinct Species, that are, as ſo many conſtituent Parts, neceſſary to the Nouriſhment and Increaſe of that ſimple Body. Therefore no Species of Trees periſhes, in as much as the Seeds, in which it lives, always remain alive, and ſhould they be received in a proper Place, forthwith they imbibe a more diſtinct Conformation, Nutrition, Augmentation, and by Degrees arrive at a due Perfection. The ſame may be ſaid of the other Species of the *Univerſe*, not only of Animals and Trees, but alſo of Stones, Minerals, and Metals, which are not leſs vegetable and organic, having their own Seeds, formed in their own Matrix, and encreaſing with a peculiar Nutriment, as well as Men, Quadrupedes, Reptiles, Birds, Fiſhes, and Plants.

VIII.

'TIS true, Philoſophers, for the moſt Part, are of Opinion, that Gold, Cryſtal, *&c.* are ſimilar, or Bodies

dies of like Nature and Parts, made up of an external Appoſition, or any other Way, becauſe they appear ſo to the Senſes. But the *Pantheiſts* think, that they conſiſt of diſſimilar Parts, from whoſe Comprehenſion, (this, or that having the Aſcendant, as a Principle of Compoſition,) ariſes the Body called *Homœomeres.* There is no ſuch Thing to be met with as a ſimilar mixed Body, no not even in Metals and Stones, for Chymiſts demonſtrate, that ſuch Bodies are cemented by a manifold growing together of ſeveral Subſtances; for which Reaſon, from Gold, than which nothing ſeems to be more ſimilar, they extract Sulphur, Quick-ſilver, Earth, and other Things, that go to the Compoſition of this noble Metal, (though not all Things, as this would exceed the Bounds of human Induſtry. In Stones and Metals we may behold ſundry Shapes of Veins, ſuch as the Shoots, as it were, of Branches and Roots, ſpread far and wide, which they have in their Mines and Quarries; from whence, (to appropriate to myſelf the Words of a certain Philoſopher) a friendly

ὁμοιομερὲς. Homœomeria. Lucr. i. 830. A Likeneſs of Parts.

ly Aliment gently* filtrates, first through Passages more lax, afterwards gradually through more narrow ones, to refine and make purer the Nutriment, and finally, an Exhalation passes through thin and hidden Pores. As the Blood flows up and down, and is driven to the Extremities of the Body, so in the Nature of Blood an alimentary Substance distills through the narrow Holes of Stones and Metals, from whence each Part, through its own Conduit, sucks in what is befitting its Nature. If such a nutricious Sap is less perceptible in them, than in the Stomach and Veins of Animals, let him remember, who requires this from Nature, that a distinct Aliment from the Parts does not appear more in Trees, whose Anatomy, notwithstanding, has been executed by several. If one should say, that in Plants there are certain Figures of a Trunk, Branches, Leaves, Blossoms, Fruit, Seeds, so also in these all this may be found, either analogous, or in a different Manner: And as Plants themselves

* *Prolectatur*, from whence, by an attractive Charm, or by Way of a Lure, *&c.* the genuine Signification of the Word.

themſelves ſhrub not after the ſame Way, why then ſhould we admire, if Things propagated under the Earth, meet with a different Kind of Life? The Man who at any Time obſerved innumerable Gems, beautifully diſtinguiſhed by various Figures, to grow in certain Places, there's no Reaſon he ſhould believe, they were leſs actuated with Life, than the Teeth and Bones of Animals. As every Country is not productive in every Thing, in like Manner, all Stones, and all Plants grow not every where; every Place affords not a proper Nouriſhment to every Particular. Marble grows here, Diamond there; one Stone puts on its due Form ſooner, another Stone later; this Seed generates Pebbles, that Rocks. Stones receive an Increaſe and Decreaſe, are more or leſs durable, as well as all other vegetative Beings. But ſome are at a Stand when they perceive no Room for Nouriſhment and Increaſe through ſuch hard Bodies, and ſuch narrow Pores. Who (ſay they) can believe that the vaſt Bulks of Stones and Metals are nouriſhed like Bones, and increaſe by Vegetation?

What

What nutricious Force can ſoften and dilate that invincible Hardneſs? But (to anſwer them by another Queſtion) what is admirable here, that we behold not alſo in the Teeth of Animals? They are harder than moſt Stones and Metals, notwithſtanding they imbibe their Aliment through minute and imperceptible Conduits, and encreaſe according to every Dimenſion. Yet that Teeth may receive the Addition of a new Subſtance, 'tis neceſſary that each Part ſhould be as firmly compacted, and diffuſed into a larger Bulk, which in like Manner would be feaſible, if a Tooth was equal to a Mountain or Iſland. If this is no Matter of Wonder with regard to Bones, and the hardeſt Trunks of Trees, why, pray, ſhould it ſeem next to a Prodigy with regard to Stones and Metals? As growing Trees and Trees hewed down differ, ſo Stones in Quarries, and Stones hewed out of them: Thoſe are alive, and theſe are dead; thoſe in their native Beds are full of Sap, theſe torn aſunder are deſtitute of Moiſture, and at length are reduced to Duſt. In a Word, every Thing in the Earth is organic,

organic, and there is no equivocal Generation, or without its own Seed, of any Thing in Nature. Wherefore it is not without Reason, that the *Earth* ſhould receive the Appellation of Mother * *Panſpermia*, to whom the *Sun* † *Pammeſtor* is a never decaying Huſband; and this juſtifies my Anſwer to a *German* Inn-keeper, who impertinently importuned me to tell him, what Countryman I was? *The Sun is my Father, the Earth my Mother, the World's my Country, and all Men are my Relations.* As if an ignorant and inſipid Perſon ſhould accoſt me with this Verſe out of *Homer*,

Τίς? πόθεν εἶς ἀνδρῶν? πόθι τοι πόλις? ἠδὲ τοκῆες?

Who? From whence are you? Where's your City? Where was you born?

* A Mixture of all Seeds.

† That influences all Things, *A Maſter*, from μῆδος, *Cura*.

IX.

THE *Pantheiſts* maintain the *Pythagoric* Aſtronomy, more properly called the *Ægyptian*, or to ſpeak with the Moderns, the *Copernican*, placing the Sun in the Center of the Planets that turn about it, among which our Earth is neither the leaſt nor the moſt inconſiderable: Like unto it, there are other innumerable Earths, making their Revolutions in ſtated Times, according to their reſpective Diſtances about their own Suns, or fixed Stars, as they call them. The ſame they ſtedfaſtly hold to, with regard to Comets that deſcribe the greateſt Circles. Good Gods! whilſt they devote themſelves to the Study of ſurveying the Heavens and the Earth, what an exquiſite Pleaſure ariſes from the everlaſting Courſes of wandering Stars? In the Contemplation of which they calculate both the Velocity of the Leſſer, and Slowneſs of the Greater, actuated with one and the ſame Motion of Nature. Hence they eaſily conclude, that

that there are no real Wanderings of the Planets, that none of them retrogrades, none of them ſtands, none of them goes out of its right Road, howſoever theſe Particulars might appear to the Eyes of Men. They alſo know exactly in what Senſe antient Connoiſſeurs underſtood the Muſic of the Spheres: *That ſo great and ſo ſweet a Sound*, ſays Cicero, *joined together by unequal Reſts, though in the exacteſt Proportion, is the Reſult of the Impulſe and Motion of the Orbs themſelves, and mingling Sharps with Flats, conſtantly produces ſeveral harmonious Concerts.* The more antient and wiſer Kind of Philoſophers underſtood this, not of a flat or ſharp Sound, not of the ſeven-fold Diviſion and Agreement of Tones, but of the wonderful Harmony of theſe Motions; whilſt Poets departing not from their Art, indulged their Fancy, and whilſt the monſtrous Forgers of ſolid Spheres grew delirious, and as a Puniſhment for their Folly, in a Manner heard the Rapidity of the Sound. How many, and what agreeable Problems are eaſily ſolved by the Pupils of the *Pantheiſts*! As among other Things, by what Means

Som Scip. Cap. v.

the ſloweſt Star can get up to the quickeſt, which is not alledged here, as a Thing difficult to be explained, but that, in a few Words, I might give ſome Hints of their Doctrine, with regard to the *Co-incidence of Extremes,* (if I'm allowed the Term) ſeeing that, purſuant to the Rules of their Inſtitutes, I am not allowed to lay open the Whole.

X.

FROM this *Co-incidence of Extremes,* the PANTHEISTS deduce a certain Third, and truly wonderful Motion of the Earth; which is to be meaſured by the Progreſs of the Equinoctial Points (the fixed ſhewing it to a Demonſtration) and therefore, by the ſlow, but continued Declination of the meridian Line. The Axis of the Earth, I ſay, rolls without ceaſing, always parallel to itſelf, about the Pole of the Ecliptic, from which it is diſtant, in every Place, twenty-three Degrees and a half, inclining to the Plane of the Ecliptic, and the Equinoxes by Degrees proceed to the ſouthern Parts, having

having nothing to do with the Ecliptic. Than this there cannot be a clearer Demonſtration, founded upon the Obſervations of *Ariſtarchus*, *Eudoxus*, *Hipparchus*, *Ptolomy*, *Copernicus*, *Halley*, and other excellent antient and modern Aſtronomers; ſo that when the Equinoxes come to the Tropic of Capricorn, there's a Neceſſity of their proceeding farther to theAntartic Pole, and ſo afterwards by turning about to the Artic. We *Britons* in reality are more remote now from the Artic Pole, than in the Time of *Pytheas* the *Maſſilian*: Although the eighth Sphere is at ſo great a Diſtance from the Earth, that the Diverſities, Magnitudes, and Oppoſitions of the celeſtial Appearances, deſcribed by antient Aſtronomers, ſeem not ſo much changed to the Senſes, throughout the Courſe of two thouſand Years and upwards; but that we have in effect come nearer to the Antartic Pole, not only the Seaſons of the Year, by little and little altered by the Progreſs of the Equinoxes, are a Teſtimony; but alſo a milder Temperateneſs of the ſame Seaſons, proceeding from hence, which

which evidently appears from Hiſtory and the Authority of Obſervations. This third Motion (which I call Equinoctial, to diſtinguiſh it from the diurnal and annual Motion of the Earth) proceeding gradually from Eaſt to Weſt, brings Matters ſo to paſs, that the Sphere, called the Eighth, or the Region of viſible fixed Stars, though immoveable, might ſeem, nevertheleſs, to go from Weſt to Eaſt; ſo that whether the eighth Sphere moves over the Poles of the Ecliptic *in Conſequentia*, or whether there is a Progreſs of the Equinoxes *in Antecedentia*, the Appearances will be the ſame, and all the ſame Things will affect our Sight. This Phænomenon ſhould be explained the ſame Way, as the other Motions of the Earth, formerly attributed to the Sun and Planets, and it muſt be reſcued from the Abſurdities of prating Cavillers, both which we have ſufficiently acquitted ourſelves of, in the third Book of *Eſoterics*.

κίνησις εἰς ἑπόμενα προήγησις ἰσημερινή.

XI.

AS a natural Conſequence of this equinoctial Motion, every Particle of our Globe, the ſame may be ſaid of the other Planets, muſt, in the Courſe of Ages, undergo all Sorts of Adventures and Viciſſitudes. *This Inclination of the Meridian,* ſays every *Pantheiſt, ſhews that the Axis of the Earth does not always paſs through oppoſite Parts. Whence it comes to paſs, that by little and little, and inſenſibly different and different Regions, are placed under the Axis, and the Inhabitants of the Zone, now frigid, are brought back and turned to the equinoctial Line; and, at length, the Place of the Artic Pole to the Antartic, and the Eaſt to the Weſt, which* Herodotus, *from the ſacred Authority and myſterious Monuments of the Ægyptian Prieſts, teſtifies to have happened formerly twice.* That is, * the Sun twice ſets

* Ἐν τοίνυν τούτῳ τῷ χρόνῳ τετράκις ἔλεγον ἐξ ἠθέων τὸν ἥλιον ἀνατεῖλαι· ἔνθα τε οὖν καταδύεται, ἐνθεῦτεν δὶς ἐπαντεῖλαι· καὶ ἔνθεν νῦν ἀνατέλλει, ἐνθαῦτα δὶς καταβῆναι. Lib. ii. Cap. 142.

ſets where it now riſes, and riſes as often where it now ſets. This not only twice, but alſo innumerable Times, has happened, and will happen in the eternal Duration of Things, although ſuch a Converſion of the Stars, and a Reduction of all Parts into the ſame Situation, requires a Revolution of about thirty-ſix thouſand Years. *Copernicus*, it ſeems, would fain reduce this Number to twenty-five thouſand Years. O how often thoſe have been made a Jeſt of, who ridiculed the *Ægyptians!* whoſe naked Bounds they even underſtood not, unſkilled in the purer Aſtronomy: I may ſafely call them barbarous Strollers, juggling and enſnaring the Minds of the little People with ſtrangely monſtrous Whims. *But from this Obſervation*, (as that moſt ingenious Man proceeds) *on which Mathematicians ſhould employ all their Care, and Study, we perceive a ſingular Underſtanding of Nature and admirable Providence, that the ſame Part of the Earth ſhould not be condemned to ſo long a Cold, but that each, and every Region, might partake in its Time, of all the Aſpects of the Sun; which, notwithſtanding, upon*

account

account of the Slowneſs of Motion, and the ſhort Life of Man is not diſcerned. That Change of the Axis might be alſo a Proof of the Force, whereby the Earth directs itſelf to a certain Part of the eighth Sphere, to paſs gradually from one to another Place of the Earth; whence there is a Neceſſity of the Climates of Regions being changed, and the Latitudes of Cities, and the Situation of Sun-dials placed upon the Meridian Line. Moreover, the Equinoctial Line of the Earth is changed with the Axis, and paſſes to another Part of the Earth; but as it is always perpendicular to the Axis, if no other Change happened, the Equinoctial Line would be ſtill found under the Star of Aries, *as it was in the Time of* Eudoxus, *and the Equinoctial Points would not have moved forward* in Antecedentia. Notwithſtanding, that this comes to paſs, it is moſt certain, for now the largeſt Star in the Horn of *Aries* (in which, in *Eudoxus*'s Time, the vernal Equinox was placed) with regard to the Ecliptic, has at leaſt the Breadth of three Degrees towards *Piſces*; but with regard to the Equator it has ſuch a Bending, that it almoſt touches the Tropic of *Cancer.* Whereſore it neceſſarily follows, that the Ecliptic is changed, which was in the Time of *Eudoxus.*

XII.

THE ſame Change, by an almoſt parallel Reaſon, holds good with regard to Fluids and Solids, Moiſture and Dryneſs; for whatever is Sea now, was formerly Land, and all that is now Land, will, in time to come, be Sea, the Bulk and Aſpect of the terraqueous Globe remaining always the ſame. This is a new Doctrine I confeſs, but a very true one; and of this Opinion, unleſs I am miſtaken, was, among other Diſciples of the *Ægyptians*, the *Clazomenian Anaxagoras*, * *who being aſked, whether the Mountains of* Lampſacum *were to be at any Time Sea? Yes, ſays he, unleſs Time ſhould fail.* For he believed, that they were partly diſcovered, and partly made

* Προς τὸ τὸν εἰποντα, εἰ τὰ ἐν Λαμψάκῳ ὄρη ἔσαι ποτὲ θαλαττα; φασὶν ἐπειπεῖν, ἐάν γε ὁ χρόνος μὴ ἐπιλείπῃ. Diog. Laert. *Lib.* ii. *Sect.* 10.

made by the Ebbing of the Sea, (as we ſhall explain elſewhere) and that they ſhould be overwhelmed and conſumed by its Flowing. Wherefore the Ocean, not without Reaſon, was called by the Antients *Amphitrite*, becauſe it environs, tears, and makes a Havock of the Earth. The Slowneſs of theſe Converſions carries a Face of Difficulty, when obſerved by ſome of the Learned; but it is by thoſe who proceed ſlowly: Whereas, if the Obſervations are made by the more ſprightly, moſt commonly they become neglected by all, if not finally entirely forgotten. *Hence it is that* Theophraſtus *dying*, (according to the Relation of *Tully) is ſaid to have accuſed Nature, for having granted a long Life to Harts and Ravens, that did not want it; and ſuch a Span to Men, to whom it would be of vaſt Conſequence to live longer; and could their Days be lengthened, all Arts and Sciences would be brought to a Perfection, and Man's Life would be improved in all Kinds of Learning. He, therefore, complained, that Death ſeized him, when he had juſt began to have a glimmering Light of theſe*

'Απὸ τοῦ ἀμφιτρέβειν ἢ ἀμφιτρέχειν.

Tuſc Diſput. Lib. 3.Cap.28.

Things. We examine not how just this Complaint is, neither do we deny the Truth of *Hippocrates*'s Maxim, **Life is short, but Art is long.* However, we are not entirely destitute of all Help to pass a Judgment upon the Equinoctial Motion, as it is evident to the Learned, that the same Points of the Earth turn no more towards the *Great Bear*, the ‡ *Lesser Bear*, and other fixed Stars, which in the Time of *Hipparcus*, or even of *Ptolomy*, had such a Situation, to say nothing of the remarkable Changes of Shores, Islands, and other Parts of our Globe, occasioned by this Vicissitude. Far be it from me, that I should assert any thing, that is not proved by Experience and Reason, it is therefore then, that I reject every precarious Hypothesis and empty Conjecture, which are denied with a better Right than projected. I discard, in like Manner, and pass the same impartial Judgment upon Things granted, and not evident or proved, and all such Fallacies, on which

* Ὁ βίος βραχὺς ἡ δὲ τέχνη μακρή. Aphorism. I. 1.

‡ Or the Star in the Tail of the *Lesser Bear*.

which very often lies the whole Streſs of a *Demonſtration.*

XIII.

BY this Ebbing or Declination of the Sea, I ſpoke of (which we allow to be more eaſily proved from the long Continuance of Time, than from Obſervation) certain Bodies can be fully accounted for, eſpecially Sea-Bodies, which are found in every Part of the Earth, and not only buried deeply, but alſo very often broken from huge Rocks, and the hardeſt Marble. That theſe are the real and identical Bones, Spoils, Remains of Fiſhes, and other Animals, the learned *Woodward*, after the Attempts of ſome others, has copiouſly demonſtrated, a Man of great Penetration in theſe Studies, and deſerving well of the learned World for his curious Obſervations, and for ſhewing that theſe are not Sports of Nature, nor Stones of their own Kind, nor terreſtrial Fiſhes or Shells, as many others have idly dreamed. We are to form no other Judgement

ment of the Scraps of Vegetables buried the ſame Way. For all Species of Stones (as we hinted above) receive their Increaſe, as well as all other Vegetables, from a looſe fluid Matter ſuitable to them, which Matter ſometimes ſhuts up within itſelf the hard and ſmall Bodies that perchance fall in its Way, or running into ſuch Bodies, if hollow, and by Degrees petrifying therein, as in a Matrix, finally aſſumes their Form. Thus it is, that we muſt likewiſe explain the Origin of figured Stones, as the * *Echites*, † *Conchites*, and all of the like Kind. *Eſoterics* furniſh us with a ready Explanation; but not the univerſal Deluge, ſuch, as there never was, the Globe of the Earth ſtill remaining, (among others, the famous *Stillingfleet*, late Biſhop of *Worceſter*, proving this clearly in his *Sacred Origins*) nor that ever it could in reality be effected by the Separation of Parts, whatever way any one ſhould take to explain it. I ſay this, with a due Deference to the Learning and

* A precious Stone of a darkiſh green Colour, and ſomewhat like a Viper.

† Stones, I ſuppoſe, formed from the Shells of Fiſhes, and reſembling Pearls.

and Reputation of *Burnet*, *Woodward*, *Whiston*, and others, who have not exactly understood the Narrative, or dived thoroughly into the Design of that wise Law-giver *Moses*, with regard to the Origin of Things, and the general Flood; not to say that the History of this *Ægyptian* Philosopher concerning the Rise, Fall, and intermediate Vicissitudes of Things, abridged afterwards by those that followed him, was superstitiously, or sillily, wrested from its genuine Signification by many, or vastly corrupted by idle Jugglers. As the Figuration of Stones is understood by the *Pantheists*, so also are the Representations of Plants, and other Things impressed upon Stones; but Trees digged out of heathy Grounds and marshy Places, are deservedly for the most attributed by them to Tempests, Inundations, Earth-quakes, and to Men who hewed them down, which I myself have very often found cut and burnt: This is evinced from proper Arguments, that cannot be now alledged; for we must not here go to the Bottom of Things, or descend to Particulars. Upon these (before recited) most solidly

Act Apost. cap. vii. ver. 22.

Burnt and scorched towards the Roots, as the Bog Firr found in *Ireland*.

laid

laid Foundations of the *immenſe and eternal Univerſe*, the *Pantheiſts* build their Philoſophy, and imbelliſh it with all poſſible Perfections. A more ſubtil Explanation of Things, and the Solutions of Phænomenons are to be met with in our *Eſoterics*, it being our Deſign to write at preſent Hiſtorically and not Phyſically.

XIV.

IT will not be amiſs to remark, as we go along, that the excellent * Author, above quoted, *upon Diet*, (whom I judge to be not *Hippocrates*, but ſome one more antient) delivered in a few Words, like ſo many Oracles, the whole Doctrine of the Revolution of all Things, the Appearances remain-ing

* Εἰ γὰρ καὶ μὴ Ἱπποκράτους ἐστὶν ἐκεῖνο τὸ βιβλίον, ἀλλ' Ζυρυφῶντος, ἢ Φαῶντος, ἢ Φιλιστίωνος, ἢ Ἀρίστωνος, ἤ τινος ἄλλου τῶν παλαιῶν· εἰς πολλοὺς γὰρ ἀναφέρουσιν αὐτό. Πάντες ἐκεῖνοι τῶν παλαιῶν ἀνδρῶν εἰσιν: ἔνιοι μὲν Ἱπποκράτους πρεσβύτεροι, τινὲς δὲ συνακμάσαντες αὐτῷ. GALEN. *de victu in acutis morbis*. *Lib.* 1. *Oper. Tom.* 5. *P.* 43.

ing always the ſame. For after having reaſoned upon the primary Elements of Nature, together with their infinite Concretions and Secretions, and deduced accurately from thence this Theorem, * *Every Thing is to All, as All is to every Thing*, he purſues his Argument in the following Words, as if delivered from a Tripode: † *Each, and every Thing, as well divine as human, is turned up and down; Days and Nights have their Increaſe and Decreaſe, ſo alſo has the Moon; there's an Acceſs of Fire and Water;* ‡ *the Sun too has various Appearances,*

G

---

* Ἕκαστον πρὸς πάντα, καὶ πάντα πρὸς ἕκαστον, τὤυτο. *Lib.* 1. *Sect.* 1.

† Χωρεῖ δὲ πάντα, καὶ θεῖα καὶ ἀνθρώπινα, ἄνω καὶ κάτω ἀμειβόμενα: ἡμέρη καὶ εὐφρόνη ἐπὶ τὸ μήκιστον καὶ ἐλάχιστον, ὡς καὶ τῇ σελήνῃ τὸ μήκιστον καὶ τὸ ἐλάχιστον. Πυρὸς ἔφοδος καὶ ὕδατος. Ἥλιος ἐπὶ τὸ μακρότατον καὶ βραχύτατον. Πάλιν ταῦτα, καὶ οὐ ταὐτά: φάος Ζηνὶ σκότος Ἅδῃ, φάος Ἅδῃ σκότος Ζηνί. Φοιτᾷ καὶ μετακινεῖται, κεῖνα ὧδε, καὶ τάδε κεῖσε, πᾶσαν ὥρην. Διαπρησσόμενα κεῖνά τε τὰ τῶνδε, τὰ δὲ ταῦτα κείνων; καὶ θ' ἃ μὲν πρήσσουσιν οὐκ οἴδασιν, ἃ δὲ πρήσσουσι δοκέουσιν εἰδέναι, καὶ θ' ἃ μὲν ὁρῶσιν οὐ γινώσκουσιν: ἀλλ' ὅμως αὐτοῖσι πάντα γίνεται δι' ἀνάγκην θείην, καὶ ἃ βούλονται, καὶ ἃ μὴ βούλονται. Φοιτεόντων δ' ἐκείνων ὧδε, καὶ τῶνδε κεῖσε, συμμισγομένων τὸ πρὸς ἄλληλα, τὴν πεπρωμένην μοίρην ἕκαστον ἐκπληροῖ, καὶ ἐπὶ τὸ μέζον καὶ ἐπὶ τὸ μεῖον. *Ibid.*

‡ That is to ſay, according to the right, oblique, or

ances, with regard to us. Again, these, and not these: Light to Jupiter *is Darkness to* Pluto, *and Light to* Pluto *is Darkness to* Jupiter. *Those come to, and are transposed here, these there, in all Times. Those pass over what belongs to these, and these what belongs to those; they know not what they do, but they seem to themselves to know what they do, and what they see they know not; but all Things are actuated in them by a divine Necessity, both what they will and what they nill. Now those coming here, and these there, and mingled through one another, every one of them satisfies its destined Fate, as well to more as to less.* When once we know, that in this remarkable Passage by *divine* celestial Bodies, are understood, and by *human* terrestrial, that *Pluto* signifies the Centre of the Earth, or of every Globe, and *Jupiter* the

or parallel Position of the Globe, it appears longer or shorter over our Horizon, or that by Solstices and Equinoxes, it produces the Vicissitudes of Seasons, and all other Changes that happen in our Globe. Whether this be a reasonable Interpretation of the Words *Sol ad longissimum & brevissimum*, must be left to the Determination of the ingenious Reader, the Translator confesses he could not fathom, to his Satisfaction, the Meaning of them.

the Surface, or circumfused Air: These, I say, being well understood, that Man will easily conceive all the rest, who, together with the mutual Access and Recess of *Moist* and *Dry*, or the Sea and Land, comprehends those Things I already inculcated, concerning the continued Declination of the Meridian Line, and consequently, concerning the not less continued, though almost imperceptible Change of the Axis of the Earth. All these Particulars duly considered, either with regard to the Variation of Particles always changing their Place, or with regard to the Constancy of never varying Appearances, the Condition of all the Globes in the infinite Ether, is alike; the Contemplation of which, is undoubtedly, not only the most agreeable, but also the most noble of all the Things that come within the Verge of true Philosophy.

XV.

THAT the Abettors of the *Universal Deluge, and general Conflagration*, ſhould not complain, that nothing is granted them; weighing Things in the Scales of *Heraclitus*,* and uſing his Form of Expreſſion, we give up to them what they deſire, and yet we do not. We ſay, that the whole Earth was overwhelmed by Waters, and it was not; and again, that all Waters ſhall be conquered by Fire, and ſhall not; but that no prepoſterous Interpretation ſhould be given to what we ſay, as it happened to that great Philoſopher, though upon a different Matter, we ſhall ſet forth more manifeſtly our Sentiments. Wherefore we maintain, that, in reality, there's no Part of the Earth, but was ſome time or other covered by Sea, and that

* Θεοὶ θνητοὶ τ' ἄνθρωποι, ἀθάνατοι ζῶντες τὸν ἐκείνων θάνατον, θνήσκοντες τὴν ἐκείνων ζωήν. Καὶ πάλιν, ποταμοῖς τοῖς αὐτοῖς ἐμβαίνομεν, εἶμεν τε καὶ οὐκ εἶμεν. HERACLIT. *de Allegor.* HOMER; but another *Heraclitus*, an Interpreter of *Homer*, called by *Heraclitus*, the Philoſopher *Obſcure*, σκοτεινός, whoſe Words we already cited.

that there is no Part of the Sea, but will be, at length, poſſeſſed by the Earth; for *Siccity* or *Dryneſs* very often, among the Writings of the Antients, has the Signification of *Fire*, of which it is both the Property and Effect. In the ſo often quoted Books upon *Diet*, we ſeveral times meet with *Fire*, in the Senſe of *Dry* or *Solid*, it being uſual with Writers to put the Effect for the Cauſe. The moſt Antient of the *Hebrews*, without any Addition, uſed *Dry* for Earth, and the moſt antient *Greeks*, *Moiſt*, abſolutely for *Sea*. So *Moſes* ſpoke, ſo † *Homer*. As therefore there is an Acceſs of *Dry*, ſo alſo there is a Receſs of *Moiſt*, interchangeably ſucceeding each other, as well in a Macrocoſm as Microcoſm. The whole Earth, I ſay, was formerly buried under Water, and the whole Sea hereafter ſhall grow dry, or, which is the ſame, ſhall turn to Fire. From which Places miſconſtrued, and

---

* וְתֵרָאֶה הַיַּבָּשָׁה et appareat aridum, &c. *Gen.* i. 9, 10. Videatur etiam *Jon.* i. 9, & ii. 10. *ac Pſal.* cvx. 5. item *Dan.* ii. 10.

† ——————— πουλὺν ἐφ' ὑγρὴν Ἤλυθον ἐς Τροίην. *Iliad* x. *ver.* 27.

and from the myſterious Words of the *Chaldeans* miſunderſtood, flowed the Prodigy of the *Univerſal* and *final Conflagration.* Now that any ſuch thing, as that either an abſolute Sway of Moiſt over Dry, or Dry over Moiſt, has ever univerſally been, or ſhall be, in one and the ſame time, or together, as it is ſaid, and at once; we not only ſimply deny it, but we prove that it is by no means poſſible. We are not ſo ſilly as to credit *Deucalionean* Fables, and *Stoical* Dreams, neither do we allow the ſuppoſed Qualities of the *Peripatetics,* which generating like ones to themſelves, can ſome time or other reduce, or rather change, all others into themſelves. * Two Theories are made out of theſe Qualities, upon the Permutation of the Four Elements, which are not Elements, as mixed, or, if they are ſimple, they are in no wiſe fit, as we before remarked, to expound the Varieties of Things, as neither is the Matter of *Des Cartes*'s firſt, ſecond, and third Elements. Nature

* Or rather the Peripatetics, by the Means of theſe Qualities, have botched up two Theories upon, &c.

ture opens a more ready way. Infinite, ſimple, and diſſimilar Subſtances, or the primary Bodies of infinite Species, moveable and indiviſible, make all the Mixtures of all Things, of which they themſelves are the eternal, unexhauſted, and immutable Matter. But the Concretions, that proceed from thence, as they have no other Production than the various Conjunctions of thoſe Bodies, ſo they have no other Deſtruction than the Separation of theſe ſame Bodies, by whatever Cauſe this falls out to be ſo. Thus it need not be apprehended that Generation ſhould at any Time fail, the firſt Subſtances remaining incorrupt, and there being always an Aſſent and Diſſent of Parts; neither, in like Manner, is it to be dreaded, that any Contrariety, whatever finally it is, ſhould convert into itſelf, or conſume the other Parts of the *Univerſe*, as there can be no Diviſion, much leſs Permutation of the firſt Bodies. Hence Chymiſts, alas! may deſpond of ever finding the Philoſopher's Stone. Therefore a conſtant and perpetual Reciprocation of all poſſible mixed Bodies follows, by which nothing

nothing is truly deſtoyed in the *Univerſe*; but, as I above mentioned, every Thing changes only its Place; for which Reaſon, though a Creation out of nothing is looked upon, by the *Hebrew* Cabaliſts, and the Philoſophers of other Nations, to be the Production of a Thing, both out of the Nothing of itſelf, and out of the Nothing of a pre-exiſting Subject, yet all Things can be ſaid to be properly *created*; for all Things, as we have ſhewn, are ſo moved, as to make appear that there is a Proceſs and Receſs *in Infinitum*: And although the Series of Motions, and the Series of all Things is eternal, yet there is no Motion, no Thing eternal, but all Things are made anew, all Things are truly created. But of this elſewhere, now what follows.

XVI.

INASMUCH as (to return now into the Circle) Philoſophy is divided by the *Pantheiſts*, as well as other antient

tient Sages, into *External*, or popular and depraved; and *Internal*, or pure and genuine; no Diſcord ariſes among them, if every one of the *Brotherhood* profeſſes the Hereſy he ſucked in with his Milk, (ſo it be not entirely falſe) or that, which has been any where eſtabliſhed. They never enter into a Diſpute upon ſcholaſtic Baubles, ſuppoſing that, in *indifferent Matters*, nothing is more prudent than the old Saying, *We muſt talk with the People, and think with Philoſophers.* But ſhould the Religion derived from one's Father, or enforced by the Laws, be wholly, or in ſome reſpects, wicked, villainous, obſcene, tyrannical, or depriving Men of their Liberty, in ſuch Caſe the *Brethren* may with all the Legality in the World, betake themſelves immediately to one more mild, more pure, and more free. They not only ſtedfaſtly aſſert and hold to a Liberty of Thought, but alſo of Action, deteſting, at the ſame time, all Licentiouſneſs, and are ſworn Enemies of all Tyrants, whether deſpotic Monarchs, or domineering Nobles, or factious Mob-leaders. Many of them are to be met

Φιλοσοφία ἐξωτερικὴ καὶ ἐσωτερική.

with in *Paris*, in *Venice* alſo, in all the Cities of *Holland*, eſpecially at *Amſterdam*, and ſome (which is ſurprizing) in the very Court of *Rome*, but particularly, and before all other Places, they abound in *London*, and have placed there the See, and, as it were, the Citadel of their Sect. 'Tis plain, I ſpeak not of the *Royal Britiſh Society*, nor of the *French Academy* of Virtuoſos, nor of any ſuch public Aſſembly. The PANTHEISTS, as I intimated, inſtituted moderate and honeſt Banquets, not luxurious and ſcandalous, not to pleaſe a nice and delicate Palate, but to bring together Friends, and reliſh the Sweets of Converſation. There is no carouſing in their Society, no Gaming at Hazard or Dice, no Piping, Dancing, Singing, Sackbut-playing Females, no Stage Player's Entertainments, or farcical Buffooneries. Learned Diſcourſes, and a-propos Jokes, are their Operas and Sweetmeats. Theſe Suppers, in a Word, are not **Apician*, or

* *Apicius*, an Epicure, who wrote a Volume of Ways and Means to provoke Appetite, ſpent a large Eſtate on his Guts, and growing poor and deſpiſed, hanged himſelf. He lived in the Time of *Nero*.

or gluttonous, but pure, ſimple, and elegant: The Table is frugal, though neat, the Furniture indifferent, though clean, and the Brow often chearful, but never lowering. Towards the End, the Waiters and Servants, as ſo many profane and illiterate Perſons, are ſhut out, and the doors being cloſely bolted, according to the Cuſtom of the Antients, the *Brethren* variouſly converſe upon various Topics. As the Bottle is in common to all, ſo alſo is Diſcourſe. Some Queſtion or other, beſides the Arguments perhaps ſtarted, is propoſed to be ſolved by the Aſſembly, as in the *Platonic Banquet*: Or, as in the *Zenophontic* each Perſon gives an Account of his Task, either impoſed upon him by himſelf, or by others. They treat of ſerious and grave Things without Contention, of ludicrous and pleaſant, without Levity: Important Diſputes are entered upon, concerning the Knowledge of the moſt worthy Things, and from Matters indifferent ariſe agreeable Interludes.

XVII.

AS to the Order that is obſerved in theſe Societies, they have a *Preſident*, whoſe Authority is the ſame as that which was formerly enjoyed by the *Greeks* and *Romans*, upon a like Occaſion. At every Meeting the Brethren of every reſpective Place are preſent, unleſs ſome or other of them is detained by Sickneſs, or is upon a Journey, or can alledge a reaſonable Excuſe for abſenting himſelf. They have, which is moſt worthy to be related and known, *A Form of celebrating the Socratic Society*, divided into three Parts, and containing the Laws, Axioms, and Maxims of the Society. We ſhall ſoon preſent the Reader with a View of it. One Part is always read in every Meeting, the Firſt uſually, or the Laſt, the *Preſident* ſolemnly reciting before, the reſt anſwering, and ſometimes bearing Chorus with him. Moſt is ſaid alternatively, according to that Verſe of *Virgil*, *Homer* firſt ſuggeſting it,

— *In*

* —— *In alternate Meaſures ſing;*
Alternate Meaſures pleaſe the Muſes
beſt. TRAPP.

But the whole *Form* is repeated on Solſtices and Equinoxes, whoſe Converſions, by the Mediation and Influence of the Sun, produce the Viciſſitudes of Seaſons, and all other Changes that happen in our Globe. The whole *Form* is alſo read at other Times, eſpecially upon the Admiſſion of a new Brother, which is never done but by the unanimous Conſent of all, although he can be diſcarded by a Majority of Votes. The *Preſidents*, to make no room for Debates in Elections, follow the Order of their Admiſſion into the Society, and in Meetings the late *Preſident* ſpeaks firſt, and the new One is the Steward of the Feaſt. They frequently interpret the *Philoſophical Canon*, which is placed in the ſecond Part of the *Form*, and deduce from it the moſt abſtruſe Theorems of Natural Philoſophy, according

* Eclog. iii. v. 59. Alternis dicetis amant alterna Camœnæ. Μουσάων θ᾽, αἳ ἄειδον, ἀμειβόμεναι ὀπὶ καλῇ. Il, i. ver. 604. Videatur et *Hymen in* APOL. v. 189.

cording to the Sentiments of the antient *Socratics*: And it is not amiſs, that it is adjuſted to the Sentiments of the modern *Socratics*, to wit, the PANTHEISTS, or their *Brethren*, as appears from Propoſitions placed on the Margin, that none ſhould make the leaſt Scruple upon any Particular, to paſs by in Silence (as I conſult Brevity) other Interpretations of ſublime Matters made by them. At ſtated Times they ruminate on the Law of Nature, that true and never deceiving *Reaſon*, (as it is exhibited in the laſt Part of the *Form*) by the Brightneſs of whoſe Rays they diſpell all Darkneſs, exempt themſelves from trifling Cares, reject all pretended Revelations, (for what Man of Senſe doubts of true ones) explode forged Miracles, unreaſonable Myſteries, ambiguous Oracles, and lay open all Deceits, Tricks, Fallacies, Frauds, old Wives Tales, whereby a thick Cloud envelops *Religion*, and a pitchy Night overſpreads *Truth*. But the *Form* now preſents itſelf.

THE

THE

FIRST PART

OF THE

FORM

Of CELEBRATING the

SOCRATIC-SOCIETY;

CONTAINING,

The MORALS and AXIOMS of the SOCIETY.

The PRESIDENT ſpeaks,

May all Happineſs await our Meeting.

The reſt anſwer,

We inſtitute a *Socratic Society*.

PRES.

May Philoſophy flouriſh.

RESP.

RESP.

And the politer Arts.

PRES.

Attend with Silence.

Let this Aſſembly, and all that is to be thought, ſpoke, and done therein, be conſecrated to Truth, Liberty, Health, the triple Wiſh of the Wiſe.

RESP.

Both now and for evermore.

PRES.

Let us be called Equals and Brothers.

RESP.

Companions too, and Friends.

PRES.

Let us baniſh Strife, Envy, and Obſtinacy.

RESP.

Let us harbour Sweetneſs, Knowledge, and Politeneſs.

PRES.

Let Jokes and Mirth be our Pleaſures.

RESP.

May the Muſes and Graces be propitious.

PRES.

We muſt not be bigotted to any one's Opinion.

RESP.

RESP.

No, not even to that of *Socrates* himſelf: And let us deteſt all *Prieſt-craft*.

PRES.

To make all Things, notwithſtanding, the more authentic, by the Sanction of proper Authors, and the beſt of Men, (without intruding though, at the ſame time, upon the Rights of Liberty) hearken unto, beloved Companions, the Words of the moſt grave Cenſor *Marcus Porcius Cato*, related by *Marcus Tullius Cicero*, that renowned Father of his Country, in the thirteenth Chapter of the Book *De Senectute*.

RESP.

We are therefore Votaries of Truth and Liberty, that we might reſcue ourſelves from Tyranny and Superſtition.

PRES.

'I always had,' ſays *Cato*, 'the greateſt 'Veneration for Companions, and it 'was therefore, in my Queſtorſhip, that 'I inſtituted Fellowſhips on the Idean 'Feſtivals of the *Great Mother*. I feaſt 'with my Companions, but very ſoberly, as ſtill there remained a certain 'Heat of Age, which gradually cooling, every thing daily became more

Cic. de Seneɛt. cap. 13.

Cybele.

'mild and temperate. Moreover, I 'esteem not so much Feasting for the 'Pleasure it gives the Body, as for the 'coming together and Conversation of 'Friends. Our Ancestors justly called 'the Sitting down of Friends at Table 'an *Entertainment*, because it tended to 'the cementing of social Life: The '*Greeks* who call it *Drinking* and *Sup*-'*ping together*, have not termed it so 'well, inasmuch as, in that respect, 'they seem to make the greatest Account 'of what should be made the least.'

Convivium.

Compotatio, Concœnatio.

R E S P.

Let *Socrates* and *Plato* be praised,
And *Marcus Cato*, and *Marcus Cicero.*

P R E S.

Let us discuss every Thing seriously,
And fill up the Chasms of Discourse
with diverting Stories.

R E S P.

Wittily, modestly, facetiously.

P R E S.

Let us search out, diligently, the Causes
of Things, that we might live
pleasantly, and die peaceably.

R E S P.

That free from all Fear,

Neither

Neither elated by Joy, nor depressed by Sadness, we might always maintain an unshaken Constancy.

PRES.

That we may also laugh to Scorn the Bugbears of the silly People, and the Inventions of crafty Knaves, let us sing an *Ennian* Strain.

PRES. & RESP.

'I value not a Straw the Augur *Marsus*, Idem de Divinat. Lib. I. Cap. ult.
'Nor strolling Quacks, nor strolling For-
'tune-tellers,
'Nor *Isiac* Soothsayers, nor Dream-Ex-
'pounders:
'They are all an ignorant Pack of
'Boobies,
'Superstitious Prophets, shameless Con-
'jurers,
'Idle, crazy, poor Vagrants. — What
'they themselves
'Have no Faith in, others forsooth must
'believe;
'From those, they promise riches to,
'they crave a Groat,
'Let them, then, from these Riches sub-
'stract the Groat,
'And restore the Remainder.'———

PRES.

Hear ſtill to (ye beſt of Friends) the ſame wiſe *Cato*, in the fourteenth Chapter of the ſame Book *De Senectute*, teaching as divinely after his Example.

RESP.

To be healthful, chearful, and happy.

PRES.

Idem de Senect. Cap. 14.

'I take a ſingular Pleaſure (*ſays he*) in 'the *Magiſterys* that have been inſtituted 'by our Predeceſſors; and in the *Diſ-*'*courſes* that, according to antient *Cuſ-*'*tom*, are made by the *Steward of the* 'Feaſt; and in the Cups, as in *Zeno-*'*phon*'s Banquet, although ſmall, * yet 'bedewed with Liquor; and in a cool-'ing Arbour in the Summer, and in 'the grateful Viciſſitude of the Sun's 'Warmth, and that of a Winter Fire. 'Theſe Pleaſures of Life I alſo ſeek 'after, in my *Sabine* Retirement, and 'conſtantly make one of the Gueſts at 'the Entertainments of my Neighbours, 'which we ſpin out till it is late in the 'Night,

* *Rorantia* in the Text, may imply Wine and Water mixed, or ſimply Water; but this anſwers not what *Horace* ſaid of Old *Cato*: *Narratur & priſci Catonis ſæpe mero caluiſſe Virtus.*

'Night, discoursing upon various To-
'pics.

RESP.

Let *Zenophon* be the Theme of our Praise;
And the rustic *Sabines* the Subject of our Imitation.

PRES.

Let us greatly feed our Minds;
But sparingly our Bellies.

RESP.

'Tis just, and good.

PRES.

Let us toast the Graces.

RESP.

Come, 'tis a sober Toast; and we shall drink it soberly.

END *of the* FIRST PART.

THE

THE

SECOND PART.

CONTAINING

The DEITY and PHILOSOPHY of the SOCIETY.

PRES.

Keep off the prophane People.

RESP.

The Coaſt is clear, the Doors are ſhut, all's ſafe.

PRES.

All Things in the World are one,
And one is All in all Things.

RESP.

What's All in all Things is GOD,
Eternal and Immenſe,
Neither begotten, nor ever to periſh.

PRES.

PRES.

In him we live, we move, and exist.

RESP.

Every Thing is sprung from him,
And shall be reunited to him,
He himself being the Beginning, and
End of all Things.

PRES.

Let us sing a Hymn,
Upon the Nature of the *Universe*.

PRES. & RESP.

'Whate'er This is, it animates all Things, Pacuvius apud Cicer. de Divinat. Lib. I. Cap. 57.
'Forms, nourishes, increases, creates;
'Buries, and takes into itself all Things:
'And the Same, of all Things is the
'Parent;
'From thence all Things, that receive a
'Being,
'Into the same are anew resolved.

Sometimes the following.

'All Things within the Verge of mor- Manil. Astronom. Lib. I. ver. 515.
'tal Laws
'Are changed. — All Climates in revol-
'ving Years
'Know not themselves; Nations change
'their Faces;
'But the World is safe, and preserves
'its All;

'Neither

'Neither increaſed by Time, nor worn
'by Age:
'Its Motion is not inſtantaneous,
'It fatigues not its Courſe. — Always
'the ſame
'It has been, and ſhall be. — Our Fa-
'ther's ſaw
'No Alt'ration, neither ſhall Poſterity:
''Tis GOD, who for ever is immutable.

PRES.

Cicero, Tuſc. Diſput. Lib. v. cap. 2.

'PHILOSOPHY, thou Guide of Life! 'thou Searcher out of Virtue! thou Ex-'peller of Vice! What, not only would 'become of us, but even, what would 'be the Life of Man without thee? 'Thou haſt founded Cities, thou haſt 'gathered diſperſed Mankind into a So-'ciety of Life. Thou haſt united them 'to each other, firſt by a Participation 'of the ſame Abode, afterwards by 'Wedlock, and finally, by a Commu-'nion of Letters and Words. Thou 'haſt been the Giver of Laws, and the 'Miſtreſs of Manners and Diſcipline. 'We have recourſe to thee, we implore 'thy Aid, we devote ourſelves entirely 'to thee. One Day ſpent well, and 'according to thy Dictates, is to be pre-

'preferred to a prevaricating Immorta-
'lity. Whose Riches should we rather
'use than thine? Thou, I say, that
'hast granted us *a perfect Tranquility*
of Life, and hast exempted us from
'the *Terrors of Death.*'

RESP.

Reason is the true and first Law,
The Light and Splendor of Life.

PRES.

'Think not, (as ye often see re- Cicero in Orat. pro S. Roscio Amerino. cap. 24.
'counted in Fables) that those who
'have been guilty of wicked Actions,
'are scared and agitated by the flaming
'Torches of Furies. Every Man's
'own Fraud, every Man's own Terror,
'disturbs him most; every Man's own
'Wickedness spurs him on to Madness;
'his own bad Thoughts, and the Con-
'science of his Mind fill him with dis-
'mal Apprehensions. These are the
'constant and domestic *Furies* of the
'Wicked.'

RESP.

To lead a happy Life Virtue alone is sufficient,
And is to itself an ample Reward.

PRES.

What's Honeſt is the ſole Good.

RESP.

Neither is there any Thing uſeful but what is laudable.

PRES.

Now, (dearly beloved *Brethren)* the Philoſophical Canon is to be diſtinctly read, it muſt be weighed attentively, and muſt ſtand the Teſt of your Judgement.

RESP.

As the Contemplation of the Nature of Things is agreeable, ſo alſo it is a moſt uſeful Science: By Attention, therefore, we ſhall weigh and judge.

PRES.

Cicero Academ. Queſt. lib. i, cap. 6, 7.

* 'The antient Philoſophers, in order 'to diſcuſs what NATURE was, divided 'it into two Things: The one *efficient*, 'the other that which is *effected*. To 'that which effects they ſuppoſed a '*Force* inherent, and to that which is 'effected, a certain *Matter*; to both not- 'with-

* 1. *Force* is in reality *Motion*; for as there's no Force without Motion, ſo the whole Force of Matter exerts itſelf by Motion. *Body* is taken ſometimes in a broad Senſe for *Matter*; but it ſignifies for the moſt Part a certain Portion of Matter, made up of many ſimple Subſtances, ſo that Matter and Body are very often confounded.

'withſtanding both inherent; for *Mat-*
'*ter* itſelf cannot cohere, unleſs con-
'tained by ſome *Force*, nor *Force* with-
'out ſome *Matter*, as every Thing is
'compelled to be ſomewhere, the Re-
'ſult of both they called a *Body*, and as
'it were a certain *Quality*.'

* 'Some of theſe *Qualities* are *origi-*
'*nal*, others *derived from them*. The
'*Original* are of one Kind and Simple:
'The *Derived from them* are various,
'and of manifold Shapes. *Air*, *Fire*,
'*Water* and *Earth* are therefore original,
'and from them ſpring the *Forms of Ani-*
'*mals*, and all thoſe Things that are ge-
'nerated from the Earth, wherefore they
'are called *Beginnings* and *Elements*, of
'which the *Air* and *Fire* have the Force
'of *moving* and *effecting* the other Parts,
'that of *receiving*, and, as it were, of
'being *paſſive*, I mean the *Water* and
'*Earth*.

* 2. The Air, Fire, Water, and Earth, are improperly taken for Elements, as we have ſhewn in the *preliminary Diſſertation*. The Water and Earth are not ſaid to be paſſive, as if abſolutely ever at reſt; but becauſe Motion in them affects not alike the Senſes, as in Fire and Air.

* 'But they imagine a certain *Matter* '*without any Species, and devoid of all* '*that Quality* to be comprised in all, 'out of which all Things are extracted, 'and by which all Things are effected, 'capable of *receiving* all, and imparting 'to them all Kinds of *Changes*, under-'going also the same *Dissolution*, not '*Annihilation*, but rather a *Reproduction* 'of Things into their own Parts, which 'can be cut and divided *in infinitum*, 'inasmuch as the minutest Thing in 'Nature can suffer a Division.'

‡ 'What's moved, moves in *Spaces*, 'which can be divided also *in infinitum*, 'and as that *Force*, which we called *Qua-*'*lity*, is so moved and agitated up and 'down, backwards and forwards, so must 'likewise all and every Part of *Matter*, 'and

* 3. *The first Matter* consists in all the indivisible Particles of every Species, by whose Conjunction and Disjunction, all mixed Bodies are made, these without ceasing are resolved into one another, saving tho' always the constituent Parts, which neither can be divided nor annihilated.

‡ 4. The Spaces of Determinations, or Boundaries, (though all Things are in a perpetual Motion, not one point in the Universe being absolutely at rest,) are the Cause that no Species of Motion is infinite, although all Motions taken together can be properly denominated an *infinite Action*.

'and thus conjointly effect the Things 'that are called *Qualia*: Out of which, 'in every *coherent and continued Nature*, '*with all its Parts*, the *World* was made; 'externally to which there's no Part of '*Matter*, nor no *Body* existing.'

* 'All the Things that are in the 'World are *Parts* of the World, and 'comprised in an *intelligent Nature*, en-'dowed with perfect *Reason*, and the 'same *Eternal*; for there's nothing 'stronger to bring it to Destruction: 'This Force they call the SOUL of the 'World, as also a MIND, and perfect 'WISDOM, and consequently GOD.'

‡ 'To this REASON they attribute, as 'it were, a certain *prudent Knowledge* of 'all the Things that are subject to it, and 'there-

* 5. The Parts of the Universe are either integrant, or constituent, no Void being placed between them, from whose Motions and Affections a truly divine Harmony arises, which cannot be dissolved by any stronger Cause, as none such exists out of the infinite Whole.

‡ 6. The Force and Energy of the Whole sometimes receives the Name of *Providence*, which so disposes celestial and terrestrial Things, that all are administred with the greatest Reason, and no room left for either Chance or Fortune, every Thing acting by a Liberty free from Co-action.

'therefore ſuppoſe, that firſt and principally it takes Care of celeſtial Things, 'and afterwards on Earth of what belongs to *Man*: This *Adminiſtration* is 'ſometimes called by them Neceſſity, 'becauſe nothing can happen contrary 'to what it has appointed, *as being a* '*fatal and immutable Continuation of the* '*everlaſting Order*. Sometimes it is 'termed Fortune, becauſe it executes 'many Things unexpectedly with regard to us, upon Account of the *Obſcurity* and our *Ignorance of Cauſes*.'

RESP.

The Nature of the Efficient, no more than that of the Effect, leaves us hereafter no room for Doubt.

PRES.

We muſt ſet forth the Praiſes of the heavenly Origin of *Souls*, infuſed into the greateſt and ſmalleſt.

PRES. & RESP.

Some think by theſe Appearances induc'd,
That to the Bees an Energy divine,
And Part of the celeſtial Mind, is giv'n;
For that a God, diffus'd thro' all the Maſs,
Pervades the Earth, the Sea, and Deep of
Air:

Hence

Hence Men, and Cattle, Herds, and ſavage Beaſts,
All at their Births receive etherial Life;
Hither again, diſſolv'd, they back return;
Nor Death takes place: but, all immortal, fly
To Heaven, and in their proper Stars reſide.

Virg. Georg. l. 4. v. 220. TRAPP.

PRES.

Let us now make honourable mention of those Men and Women among the Antients, who taught or acted nobly.

RESP.

That they may benefit us by their Example, as well as Learning.

PRES. The sacred Memory of

SELOMO
THALES
ANAXIMANDER
XENOPHANES
MELISSUS
OCELLUS
DEMOCRITUS
PARMENIDES
DICÆARCHUS
CONFUCIUS
CLEOBULINA
THEANO
PAMPHILA
CERELLIA
HYPATIA

RESP. May it tend to our Advantage.

SOCRATES, PLATO, XENOPHON, CATO, and CICERO, have been praised in the First Part of the FORM.

PRES.

Let us praise all other philosophical Companies, and commemorate the Male and Female Votaries of Truth.

RESP.

RESP.

Let the praiſe-worthy be praiſed and honoured.

PRES.

Let us toaſt the MUSES.

RESP.

Come, we'll drink it moderately.

END *of the* SECOND PART.

THE

THE

THIRD PART:

CONTAINING

The LIBERTY of the SOCIETY;

AND

A LAW, neither deceiving, nor to be deceived.

PRES.

We muſt always wiſh,
That there ſhould be a *ſound Mind*, in a *ſound Body*.
And as *Life* is not to be laid down on a ſlight Pretext,
So *Death* is never to be dreaded.

RESP.

Nothing more is to be wiſhed for.
And to effect this, we muſt uſe our utmoſt Endeavours.

PRES.

PRES.

Let us therefore ſing joyfully and tuneably.

PRES. & RESP.

The Man in conſcious Virtue bold, Hor. lib. iii. Od. 3. v. 1.
Who dares his ſecret Purpoſe hold,
Unſhaken hears the Croud's tumultuous cries,
And the impetuous Tyrant's angry Brow defies.

Let the loud Winds, that rule the Seas,
Their wild tempeſtuous Horrors raiſe;
Let Jove's dread Arm with Thunder rend the Spheres,
Beneath the Cruſh of Worlds undaunted he appears. FRANCIS.

PRES.

Among the Wiſe
Mirth is more eſteemed than Gain.

RESP.

Mirth is the Characteriſtic of a Freeman,
Sadneſs that of a Slave.

PRES.

'Tis better to *rule over* none, than to be any Man's *Slave*.

RESP.

One may live honourably without a *Servant*;
But there's no living at any Rate with a *Master*.

PRES.

But 'tis necessary to obey the Laws,
For without them there's no Property, no Safety.

RESP.

We are therefore *Servants* of the Laws,
That we may be *Free*.

PRES.

There's as wide a Difference between *Liberty* and *Licentiousness*.

RESP.

As between *Liberty* and *Slavery*.

PRES.

Hear, therefore, (noble Equals) consider with yourselves, and always shew in your Actions, the unerring Rule for living well, dying happily, and doing all Things properly. A Rule, I say, not to be deceived, and a Law never deceiving, to be delivered to you now, in the very Words, in which formerly *Marcus Tullius* inimitably expressed it.

RESP.

RESP.

With open Ears,
And Hearts erect, we shall listen.

PRES.

'Right Reason is the only *true Law*, 'a Law befitting Nature, extended to 'all, consistent with itself, and ever-'lasting. A Law that invites Men to 'their Duty by commanding, and de-'ters from Fraud by forbidding. A 'Law that commands or forbids not in 'vain the Honest, and, on the contrary, 'by commanding or forbidding moves 'not the Dishonest. Cic. de Repub. lib. iii. Lactant. lib. vi. cap. 8.

'Tis not lawful to * obrogate this 'Law, nor derogate any thing from it, 'nor wholly abrogate it. Neither can 'we, by the Senate or People, be ex-'empted from this Law.

'We are not to seek for any other 'Explainer, or Interpreter of this Law, 'but itself; it is not a different Law at '*Rome*, from what it is at *Athens*, nor 'different now, from what it shall be 'hereafter: But one and the same Law, 'eternal

* To propose the Enacting of a Law, contrary to a former, or some Clause thereof. The Sense of *Obrogo*.

'eternal and immortal, has and ſhall 'contain all Times and Nations.

'There ſhall be one, as it were, com-'mon Maſter and Ruler of All, that GOD, the Inventor, Umpire, and 'Giver of this Law: He who obeys 'not this Law is his own Enemy, he 'ſcorns the Nature of Man, and there-'fore ſhall undergo the greateſt Puniſh-'ments, though he eſcapes all other 'ſuppoſed ones.'

RESP.

We are willing to be brought up, and
governed by this Law,
Not by the lying,
And ſuperſtitious Fictions of Men.

PRES.

Laws framed by Men, are neither clear,
nor univerſal;
Nor always the ſame, nor ever efficacious.

RESP.

They are therefore uſeful to few, or
Wholly to none.
Interpreters alone excepted.

PRES.

Be ſtill attentive.

De Divinat. lib. ii. cap. ult. 'SUPERSTITION, ſays *Tully*, (whoſe 'Words are unqueſtionably true) over-ſpreading

' ſpreading Nations, ſeized upon almoſt ' the Minds of all, and took Poſſeſſion ' of the Weakneſs of Men. This is ' evident from my Books upon the *Na-* ' *ture of the Gods*, and I have cleared it ' up to my utmoſt, in this Diſpute upon ' *Divination:* For I flattered myſelf, ' that I ſhould conduce not a little to ' my own particular Advantage, and ' that of my Country, if I could find ' a Means to root it out intirely. Not ' that it ſhould be underſtood, that by ' deſtroying Superſtition, Religion is alſo ' deſtroyed, for it is a wiſe Man's Bu- ' ſineſs to uphold the Inſtitutions of his ' Anceſtors, and retain their Rites and ' Ceremonies; but what I intimate is, ' that the Beauty of the World, and ' Order of heavenly Things, force us to ' confeſs, that there exiſts an excellent ' and *Eternal Nature*, which ſhould be ' the Object of the Contemplation and ' Admiration of all Mankind. Where- ' fore, as the *Religion* is to be propa- ' gated, that's joined to the Knowledge ' of *Nature*, ſo all the Roots of *Super-* ' *ſtition* are to be plucked out, and caſt ' away.

RESP.

RESP.

The ſuperſtitious Man, aſleep or awake, enjoys no Repoſe:
He lives not happily,
Nor dies ſecurely,
Who, living and dying,
Is a Prey to ſilly Prieſts.

PRES.

Whatever Time, Nature has allotted every Man for Life,

RESP.

He ſhould be ſatisfied with it.

PRES.

He who dreads what cannot be avoided, can never poſſeſs a ſedate Mind.

RESP.

But he who fears not Death, becauſe neceſſary, prepares a Safe-guard for a happy Life.

PRES.

As our Birth brought us the Beginning of all Things, ſo ſhall our Death the End.

RESP.

As nothing of theſe belonged to us before our Birth, ſo nothing ſhall after Death.

PRES.

He's as great a Fool who weeps;

He

He ſhall not be alive a thouſand Years hence.

RESP.

As he who weeps,
That he has not lived to a thouſand Years.

PRES.

To Fame, and Cuſtom only,
Funeral Pomps and Solemnities ſhould be granted,

RESP.

They are therefore to be deſpiſed by us;
But not to be neglected.

PRES.

Let's toaſt ſome Health.

RESP.

Come.

PRES.

My humble Service to the SOCIETY.

RESP.

It ſhall go round in full Bumpers.

PRES.

Let the new Preſident give Orders for all other Particulars.

RESP.

It ſhall be done.

Afterwards they feaſt temperately, *teaching one another and learning*, which is the Symbol and principal Scope of the Society.

END *of the* THIRD PART.

The

The two last Stanzas, taken from Horace, *inserted in the last Part of the Form, are not always chanted, other Odes of the same Poet are also sung entirely, adapted to the various Circumstances of Times and Things, as it seems proper to the* PRESIDENT. *Such are those that are conducive to Wisdom, an even Temper, the Reformation of Life, Mirth and Innocence, as in a particular manner the following.*

Vides ut alta stet nive candidum Lib.1.Od.9.
Quid dedicatum poscit *Apollonem* Ibid.Od.31.
Nullus argento color est, avaris Lib.2.Od.2.
Æquam memento rebus in arduis Ibid.Od.3.
Rectius vives, *Licini*, neque altum Ibid.Od.10.
Eheu fugaces, *Postume*, *Postume*; Ibid.Od.14.
Jam pauca aratra jugera regiæ Ibid.Od.15.
Otium Divos rogat in patenti Ibid.Od.16.
Non ebur neque aureum Ibid.Od.18.
Odi profanum Vulgus, & arceo Lib.3 Od.1.

bid.Od.2. Anguſtum, Amici, Pauperiem pati
bid.Od.23. Cœlo ſupinas ſi tuleris Manus
Ibid.Od.24. Intactis opulentior
Lib.4.Od.7. Diffugere nives, redeunt jam gramina campis
Ibid.Od.12. Jam veris comites, quæ mare temperant,
Epod. 2. Beatus ille qui procul negotiis,
Ibid. 12. Horrida tempeſtas cœlum contraxit & imbres.

Of a Two-fold

PHILOSOPHY

OF THE

PANTHEISTS,

That ſhould be followed.

To which is ſubjoined,

A ſhort DISSERTATION upon the Idea of the beſt and moſt accompliſhed MAN.

I.

WE have, in the *preliminary Diſſertation*, with as much Conciſeneſs, as Perſpicuity, diſcuſſed the Nature, Regulation, and Names of private *Societies*, or learned Entertainments among the *Greeks* and *Romans*; and, at the ſame time, we have not con-

concealed the State or Origin of the modern *Socratic Society*, which we made the chief Subject of our Discourse. By the extraordinary Form of this Society, now first brought to Light, any one may see plainly that the Manners of the *Brethren* are not morose, rather, polite and elegant, nay even devoid of all Vice and just Censure. Moreover the Laws of this agreeable Banquet, not less just than prudent, are to be learned; and the attractive Charms of Liberty, far remote from all Licentiousness, are to be thoroughly read, so much the more, as nothing is so prized by the *Brotherhood*, as not only the cultivating of Modesty, Continence, Justice, and all Kinds of Virtues themselves, but also of exciting others, as well by Words as Example, to their Practice. But they treat of all these human Things humanely. *You shall have Jokes without Gall, and Liberty not to be dreaded in the Morning, and no Restraint laid upon your Tongue.* You may perceive, that their Religion is simple, clear, easy, without Blemish, and freely bestowed, not painted over, not intricate, embarrassed, incomprehensible,

Martial. lib. 10. Epig. 48. *Accedent sine felle joci, nec mane timenda Libertas, & nil quod tacuisse velis.*

henſible, or mercenary; not luring Minds with ſilly Fables, and enſnaring them by the Filth, Inhumanity, or Ridicule of Superſtition; not ſubſervient, I ſay, to the private Advantage of any Family, or Faction, againſt the public Good; not ſcandalizing or railing at, much leſs diſturbing or tormenting any Perſon or Perſons, ſo that they be honeſt and peaceable Men. There is no Occaſion to make a longer Diſcourſe upon the Improvement of the Mind. The PANTHEISTS can deſervedly be ſtiled the * *Myſts* and † *Hierophants* of Nature; for as formerly the ‡ *Druids, Men of an elevated Genius, kept up to the Strictneſs of their brotherly Union, (as the Authority of* Pythagoras *has decreed) ſo alſo they were verſed in the Knowledge of the moſt abſtruſe Things, and their Minds were lifted up by the Contemplation of the ſublimeſt Myſteries.* The *Socratic Companions* ſtrenuouſly ruminate upon the ſame Studies, for which the *Druids* and *Pythagorics* made themſelves

---

* Prieſts; thoſe that are learned themſelves, or inſtruct others in the Myſteries of Religion.

† An Interpreter of ſacred Myſteries.

‡ Ammian. Marcellin. lib. 15. cap. 9.

ſelves ſo illuſtrious, both inſtituted Societies, yet the *Pantheiſts* allow not all their Words and Deeds; for where they depart from Truth, there we alſo depart from them, praiſing voluntarily what we approve of, and giving Thanks to thoſe, by whoſe Labour we have in any Shape benefited ourſelves.

II.

BUT perhaps it may be imputed as a Fault to the PANTHEISTS for embracing two Doctrines, the one *Ex-*
Exoterica. *ternal* or popular, adjuſted in ſome Meaſure to the Prejudices of the People, or to Doctrines publickly authoriſed for
Eſoterica. true; the other *Internal* or philoſophical, altogether conformable to the Nature of Things, and therefore to Truth itſelf: And moreover for propoſing this ſecret Philoſophy, naked and entire, unmasked, and without any tedious Circumſtance of Words, in the Receſſes of a private Chamber, to Men only of conſummate Probity and Prudence. But what Perſon, unleſs equally ignorant of the

the Disposition of the human Genius, and what's transacted in Nature, doubts that they act wisely? The Reason of what I say is manifest. For no Religion, no Sect, can brook a Contradiction, much less can endure that their Doctrines should be charged with Error or Falsity, and their Ceremonies with Vanity or Folly. All Things (an't please you) are sent down to them from Heaven, although they gape after earthly Desires. They are divine (if you credit them) and indispensably necessary for the Regulation of Life, although 'tis evident that they are human, empty also, and superfluous, and often monstrous Fictions: Nay even, for the most Part, destructive to the common and public Tranquility, as it appears to a Demonstration from daily Experience. Amongst so many various and disagreeing Opinions, if it is not possible that none of them should be true, at least it is impossible that more than one of them should be true: This is an acute Observation long ago made by *Tully, in discussing the Nature of the Gods.* Wherefore the PANTHEITS, Persons of the strictest Mode- Lib I. cap. 6.

 ration,

ration, behave towards frantic, foolish, and stuborn Men, as fond Nurses do towards their babbling Minions, who imbibe from them the pleasing Infatuation of imagining themselves Kings and Queens, that they are the only Papa and Mama's Pets, and that there are none so pretty and so finy as they. Those who flatter not Infants in these Trifles are odious and disagreeable to them. Those, on the other Hand, who
exactly *ad amussim.* do adhere not by Line and Level to the Opinions of the Ignorant, though Adults, are abominated and ill used; their Inveteracy is brought to such a Pitch, that they deign not to keep them Company, they oblige them with no Office of Humanity, they would fain have them, whilst alive, prohibited Fire and Water,
banished. and, when dead, eternally tormented. But as *Superstition* is always the same in Vigour, though sometimes different in Rigour, and as no wise Man's Attempt was amiss in rooting it out of the Minds of all Persons, which could not be compassed at any Rate; yet he'll use his Endeavours to do all that can be done, that is, by plucking out the Teeth and paring the

the Nails of this worſt and moſt pernicious of Monſters, he will not ſuffer it at its Pleaſure to hurt on every Side. It is to Men in Power, and Politicians actuated with this noble Diſpoſition of Mind, that we are indebted for all the *religious Liberty*, that is any where now a Days to be met with, which has redounded not a little to the great Advancement of Letters, Commerce, and Civil Concord. Whereas, on the contrary, to the Superſtitious, or pretended Worſhippers of Supreme Powers, I mean, to ſpirit-haunted Enthuſiaſts, or ſcrupulouſly Pious, are owing all Feuds, Animoſities, Mutinies, Mulcts, Rapines, Stigmates, Impriſonments, Baniſhments, and Deaths. Thus it neceſſarily muſt happen, *That one Thing ſhould be in the Heart, and in a private Meeting; and another Thing Abroad, and in public Aſſemblies.* This Maxim has often been greatly in Vogue, and practiſed not by the Antients alone; for to declare the Truth, it is more in Uſe among the Moderns, although they profeſs it is leſs allowed.

III.

HAVING thus briefly eſtabliſhed the two-fold Philoſophy of the Antients, it will be no difficult matter to underſtand, that the PANTHEISTS, among ſo many different Sects in Vogue, and their mutual Scuffles, I wiſh not Maſſacres and Carnage, lead a peaceable Life, and neither hurried away by a Love for thoſe, nor a Hatred for theſe, ſtudy the Safety of the Republick, and the common Good of Mankind, ſworn Enemies of all Debates and Parties. If thoſe who are going aſtray, are pleaſed to be put upon the right Road, they will courteouſly point it out to them; if they perſiſt in their Error, they will, notwithſtanding, friendly and from their Hearts exerciſe a Commerce of Life with them. They know, and lay it down for a Principle, that no Man is to be diſdained or ſcorned upon Account of indifferent and harmleſs Opinions, and that whatever Nation or Religion he is of, his Company, for the Virtues and Excel-

Excellencies of his Mind, is to be ſought for, and in no wiſe to be avoided, but for his Vices, and the Corruption of his Morals. Therefore a *Pantheiſt* will never puniſh or diſgrace any Man for a mere Sentiment; for Sayings, I ſay, or Actions that hurt no Man, neither will he adviſe or inſtigate others to deſile themſelves by ſuch a notorious Piece of Villainy. Fraudulent Prieſts, or impotent ſilly Women, may ſtir up Magiſtrates againſt them, not able at the ſame time to lay any Crime to their Charge, or upbraid them with any Thing, except that they cannot ſolve their Objections, or becauſe they live a Life more agreeable to the Dictates of Reaſon, and more uprightly than they themſelves do. But none in a public Employ, or charged with the Intereſt of the Public, will give Ear to theſe brain-ſick fantaſtic Perſons, unleſs he is a Man blinded by Superſtition, or, on the other Hand, a Slave to Ambition and filthy Gain, and conſequently regardleſs of the Honour that is due to Virtue and Merit. As for the reſt, the *Socratic Companions* laying no Streſs upon

upon the Praiſe and Scandal of others, make it their total Endeavour to live after their own, and not another's Fancy, contented with their Lot: They correct their Hearts with virtuous Precepts, and embelliſh their Minds with Learning, the better, and with greater Eaſe, to be ſerviceable to themſelves, their Friends, and all Perſons; to approach, moreover, (though they ſhould never attain to it) with more Certainty, and nearer to that Perfection, which every good and learned Man is obliged to have at Heart, and wiſh for, either to acquire it for himſelf, or impart it to others. *Cicero*, to whom our Society is indebted for ſo many, and ſuch excellent Things, towards the End of his Firſt Book *of Laws*, has furniſhed us with *A diſtinct, and exact Idea of the beſt and moſt accompliſhed Man*. Let the Learned then read, and form themſelves according to this Rule.

IV.

'HE that knows himſelf, (ſays 'Tully) will firſt ſuppoſe that 'he has ſomething Divine, and he will 'think in himſelf, that his Genius is 'conſecrated like any Image of Wor-'ſhip; and he will always act and think 'in a Manner worthy of ſo great a Fa-'vour of the Gods.

Knowlege of one's ſelf.

'And when he has throughly known, 'and wholly proved himſelf, he will 'underſtand how Nature has ſet him 'off for Life, and what conſiderable 'Means he has to obtain and acquire '*Wiſdom*, inaſmuch as, at firſt, he im-'bibed in his Mind, an imperfect 'Knowledge of all Things, adorned by 'which, and guided by *Wiſdom*, let 'him ſhew himſelf, according as his 'Soul makes a greater Progreſs towards 'Perfection, a better Man, and, as a 'neceſſary Conſequence of his Good-'neſs, let him contemplate his Happi-'neſs.

The Faculties of the Mind.

Ideas and Notions.

For

For when his Mind, formed by 'the Knowledge and Practice of Virtue, 'has quitted its Fondneſs and Indulgence for the Body, has laid a Reſtraint upon Pleaſure, as a Stain to 'Beauty, has made void the Terrors of 'Death and Pain, has entered into a 'Society of Love with its own, has reputed all its own, whom Nature has 'united by a mutual Benevolence, has 'embraced the true Worſhip of the

Religion. 'Deity, and the Purity of Religion, 'and has ſharpened the Edge as well of 'the Wit as Eyes, to chooſe Good and 'reject the contrary, (which Virtue, 'from its Forecaſt, is called *Prudence)*, 'What Situation can be ſaid or thought 'to poſſeſs a more extenſive Happineſs?

Phyſicks. 'The ſame accompliſhed Man, when 'with due Conſideration he has taken a 'View of the Heavens, Earth, Seas, 'the Nature of all Things, the Cauſes 'of their Generation, where they run 'back again, when, and how, they 'are to be diſſolved, what is mortal and 'periſhable in them, what divine and 'heavenly: When he has almoſt laid 'hold of the *Being* that rules and go-

'verns

verns theſe Things, when he has diſcovered himſelf to be not incloſed within one Wall, the Native of any circumſcribed Place, but a Citizen of the whole World, as one City: In this magnificent Appearance of Things; and in this Contemplation and Knowledge of Nature, ye immortal Powers! how well he ſhall know himſelf! (an Advice imparted to us by the *Pythean* Apollo) how he ſhall deſpiſe, ſcorn, and repute as nothing, what commonly is deemed the Height of Pomp and Grandeur! Coſmopolity.

'As by a Kind of Rampire, he'll fortify all theſe Particulars with ſtaunch Arguments, a juſt Diſcernment of Truth and Falſhood, and a certain Science and Art of Underſtanding: He'll know what Concluſions he is to draw from his Premiſſes, and what is repugnant to every Thing. Logick.

'As he's ſenſible, that he is born for civil Society, he will not only enter into the Diſcuſſion of theſe Matters, by the Subtilities of Diſpute, but alſo by a continued Diſcourſe, by which he may rule People, eſtabliſh Laws, Politics and Eloquence.

The Administration of the Commonwealth. ‘ chaſtiſe the Wicked, defend the Good, ‘ praiſe illuſtrious Men, deliver whole‘ſome Precepts and perſwaſive Encomi‘ums to his Citizens, exhort to Honour, ‘ recall from Wickedneſs, comfort the ‘ afflicted, and exhibit, by everlaſting History. ‘ Monuments, the Tranſactions and Or‘donances of the Brave and Wiſe, to ‘ the indelible Diſgrace of the Wicked.

The greateſt Wiſdom. ‘ Now as ſo many and ſuch mighty ‘ Things are perceivable in Man, by ‘ thoſe who are willing to know them‘ſelves, we muſt neceſſarily conclude, ‘ that Wiſdom is both their Parent, and ‘ the Nurſe that trains them up.’

V.

BUT who is it, that would not be willing to be more wiſe and better? Who is it that could not? And where's the End of any Diſcipline, but to make Men wiſe and good? If it is deficient in theſe Reſpects, it ſeems to me for the greater Part uſeleſs, though not entirely for Ornament and Elegance Sake to be rejected. Wherefore the

PAN-

PANTHEIST become wiſe, or at leaſt poſſeſſed of the next Degree to Wiſdom, ſhall not, in the firſt Place, to his Prejudice, run counter to the received *Theology*, that in philoſophical Matters ſwerves from Truth; neither ſhall he be altogether Silent, when a proper Occaſion preſents itſelf; yet he ſhall never run the Riſque of his Life, but in Defence of his Country and Friends. As to the moſt Holy Maxims of the *Meſſias*, which are ever, and always to be profeſſed, though without baſe Additions, and ſiniſtrous Interpretations, we undertake not to ſpeak of them here, the Place being foreign to them. Secondly, all the Truths that the *Pantheiſt* can with Safety diſcloſe, as Politics, Aſtronomy, Mechanics, OEconomics, and ſuch like, he ſhall not only not envy them to others, but even voluntarily communicate them, ſtill never without a due Caution, becauſe the Commonalty weighs moſt Things in the Scales of Opinion, and but very few in thoſe of Truth. Finally, he ſhall exactly Eſtimate, and in the Silence of his Heart, meditate upon the more ſacred Dogms, regarding either the Nature of *God*, or of the *Soul*; and he ſhall not make the Wicked, nor the Ignorant, nor any, except the Brethren alone, or other ingenious, upright, and learned Men, Partakers of *Eſoterics.* I am conſcious to myſelf, that this Silence, and prudent Reſervedneſs of Mind, will not be agreeable to all Perſons; however the PANTHIESTS ſhall not be more open, 'till they are at full Liberty to think as they pleaſe, and ſpeak as they think.

VI.

PERHAPS, one more curious, than conſiderate, ſhould aſk, whether in Effect ſuch a Society exiſts? Whether the Form we exhibited is there recited? Or rather, as ſome have projected for Models, the beſt of Kings, and the beſt regulated Commonwealths, ſo to the Image of the moſt agreeable and learned Society, all theſe Things have been framed concerning the *Pantheiſts*? Perhaps, good Sir, and what then, prithee, if the Thing is ſo? Figure to yourſelf, that

Zenophon in the Inſtitution of *Cyrus*, and *Plato* in his *Republic*.

that they are not true, notwithstanding you must acknowledge them to be probable. They are all consistent with themselves, as in the most undoubted Matters. Or, if you are willing to have a Mixture of Truth and Falshood, you may judge that those who read this *Socratic* Assembly, shall reap no less Advantage from it, than from the Chorus of *Horace*, as it commands Virtue, and forbids Vice.

Bridles wild Rage, loves rigid Honesty, Art of Poetry, v 196.
And strict Observance of impartial Laws,
Sobriety, Security, and Peace,
And begs the Gods to turn blind Fortune's
Wheel,
To raise the Wretched, and pull down the
Proud.

Lord ROSSCOMMON.

If a Person in Poetry, or Painting, should frame to himself a Mistress adorned with all possible Beauties and Graces, though in reality he's not in the Possession of such a one, yet he will not be thought to be devoid of Love, or averse from Beauty: But to clear up the

the Matter in one Word, there are, undoubtedly, in ſeveral Places, not a few *Pantheiſts*, who, according to the Cuſtom of others, have their private Aſſemblies and Societies, where they feaſt together, and what is the ſweeteſt Kind of Sauce, where they philoſophiſe over it. Whether or no that *Form* or any *Part* of it is always, and every where recited among them, I leave undecided. for your Part, Reader, whoever you are, make uſe of it, and I heartily wiſh, that it may tend to your Advantage.

F I N I S.